creative
Tabletop Fountains

creative
Tabletop Fountains

30 Projects to
Renew Your Spirit

Marthe Le Van

LARK BOOKS

A Division of Sterling Publishing Co., Inc.
New York

ART DIRECTOR: Tom Metcalf
PHOTOGRAPHER: Sandra Stambaugh
COVER DESIGN: Barbara Zaretsky
ILLUSTRATIONS: Orrin Lundgren
PRODUCTION ASSISTANCE: Amanda A. Robbins
ASSISTANT EDITOR: Veronika Alice Gunter
EDITORIAL ASSISTANCE: Rain Newcomb
EDITORIAL INTERN: Anne Wolff Hollyfield, Nathalie Mornu
PROOFREADER: Diane Weiner

Library of Congress Cataloging-in-Publication Data

Le Van, Marthe.
    Creative tabletop fountains: 30 projects to renew your spirit/ by Marthe Le Van.
        p. cm.
    Includes index.
    ISBN 1-57990-289-8
    1. Tabletop fountains. I. Title.
TT899.74.L428 2002
745.593–dc21

                        2001038648

10 9 8 7 6 5 4 3 2 1
First Edition

Published by Lark Books, a division of Sterling Publishing Co., Inc. 387 Park Avenue South New York, N.Y. 10016

© 2002, Lark Books

Distributed in Canada by Sterling Publishing, c/o Canadian Manda Group, One Atlantic Ave., Suite 105 Toronto, Ontario, Canada M6K 3E7

Distributed in Australia by Capricorn Link (Australia) Pty Ltd., P.O. Box 704, Windsor, NSW 2756 Australia

Distributed in the U.K. by Guild of Master Craftsman Publications Ltd., Castle Place 166 High Street, Lewes, East Sussex, England, BN7 1XU.
Tel: (+44) 1273 477374 • Fax: (+44) 1273 478606
Email: pubs@thegmcgroup.com • Web: www.gmcpublications.com

If you have questions or comments about this book, please contact:
Lark Books
67 Broadway
Asheville, North Carolina 28801
(828) 236-9730

Printed in Hong Kong

Contents

"When you hear the splash of water drops that fall into the bowl, you will feel that all the dust of your mind is washed away." Rikkyu (1521-1591)

Soothing our spirits as we move through a fast-paced world, tabletop fountains are more than a passing trend. As an accent piece for your living room, den, deck, or bedroom, a tabletop fountain makes a direct and attractive visual statement. It also creates a pleasant and relaxing ambience. Water has a renewing energy that we cherish: the sight and sound of water in motion is an experience deeply connected to human nature. As it flows forward in continual change, water can be a metaphor for the ebbs and flows in our lives. This successful combination of style and substance may be what makes tabletop fountains so appealing. Today, more and more people are making their own, creating unique environments where running water can work its magic as an object of beauty and an agent of calm.

Making a fountain exercises both sides of your brain: you'll receive a great workout for your imagination and build your construction skills. Fountain building is highly rewarding, no matter how much time and labor you choose to invest. The projects in this book run the gamut from simple assembly, where aesthetic decision-making is the primary challenge, to more complex constructions, where various fabrication skills come into play. There are quick-and-easy fountains, such as the Parlor Fountain on page 53; moderately challenging fountains, such as Slate Passage on page 83; and significantly more complex constructions, such as the Copper

introduction

Washboard Fountain on page 112. Whether you're making your first fountain or looking for fresh ideas, new techniques, and more challenging opportunities, you're sure to be satisfied with the variety of projects.

Among the featured fountains you'll find an exciting blend of techniques. You can build new skills to add to your craft repertoire. The Mosaic Fountain on page 60 teaches you how to adhere tumbled ceramic shards. Several projects require the use of a drill, so you'll learn how to safely and successfully make holes in slate, ceramics, bamboo, shells, and metal. Permanently attaching fountain pieces is often an important step, and this book shows many options. When constructing the Daisy Dream fountain on page 119, you'll have the chance to work with mortar. The Harmony Fountain on page 56 requires simple soldering skills. Many projects, such as the Love Eternal Fountain on page 86 and Panda Paradise on page 102, are simply glued with waterproof epoxy.

As you browse the project pages you'll notice an inspiring assortment of materials. Some simple fountain designs rely on your scavenging instinct to hunt and gather supplies. Exact matches may be elusive, but substitutions are warmly welcomed and easy to find. If you want to select an object of a different color, size, shape, or finish, go right ahead! Experiment! Let your imagination flow like water over smooth stones! As you tackle more complex projects, you'll have to fabricate many key fountain elements yourself. To achieve this, you'll need to follow longer instructions that require specific materials, as well as precise measurements and assembly procedures. Your reward for the extra time and effort you spend will be the distinct satisfaction of building an artwork from scratch.

From the subdued to the surprising, the fountains in this book extend beyond tradition. Many designs rightfully celebrate the beauty of natural elements by using such timeless items as rocks, slate, and bamboo. Other fountains feature the urban textures of glass, plastic, and metal. Whether you're drawn to warm desert tones or a cool ocean palette, rugged chiseled edges or a smooth polished shine, you're sure to find plenty of appealing projects. There are even two temporary fountains you can make for special occasions. The Avalon Ice Fountain on page 71 and the Tropical Fruit Fountain on page 90 are creative centerpieces that will astound guests at your next party, and live on in your memory.

In the basics chapter, you'll find all the necessary information to get started, plus timesaving and troubleshooting tips. There are also special interest sections on related topics, such as Suiseki, acoustics, and Feng Shui. You can learn the fundamentals of fountain making in a single afternoon but, as many enthusiasts will attest, you'll enjoy expanding your knowledge for a lifetime. There are fantastic opportunities, especially on the internet, for you to have an ongoing dialogue with other fountain makers. These forums are full of ideas and solutions you can use to grow as a fountain maker. To have a deeply satisfying creative experience making tabletop fountains, you're encouraged to experiment and take risks. Measure success not only by what you see as the end result, but also by what you have learned about fountains and yourself along the way.

getting started

Only four supplies are essential to create a table-top fountain, and you're likely to already have two on hand—water and electricity. The other two, a container and submersible pump, are easy to acquire. Building a simple fountain out of just these four elements is a great way to begin your creative journey. Fountain building is a process of continual exploration and understanding. Even for experienced artists, a return to the basics to watch the simple beauty of water and to hear its sound is inspiring. If you've got your first pump and, like most beginners, you're eager to get started, here's a quick exercise that will show you how fountains work.

*Read the directions that came with the pump. Some assembly may be required, such as attaching the pump spout and suction cup feet.

*Locate a waterproof container that's at least 2½ inches (6.4 cm) deep with a flat base. An ordinary casserole dish or mixing bowl is fine.

*Adjust the pump's water flow regulator (if it has one) to its lowest pressure setting.

*Position the pump in the center of the container. If available, use the pump's suction cup feet to lock it in place.

the basics

* Fill the container with enough tap water to cover the pump's intake valve, approximately 1½ to 2 inches (3.8 cm to 5 cm).

* Plug the pump cord into a regular electrical outlet to start the flow of water.

* Increase the pump pressure to higher levels, and observe both the sight and sound of the circulating water at each new setting.

* Unplug the cord to stop the pump, and congratulate yourself—you've just made your first tabletop fountain!

fountain elements

If the mixing-bowl-and-exposed-pump aesthetic isn't exactly what you had in mind for your living room, you'll have to delve a little deeper into the technical realm of tabletop fountains. Fortunately, the need-to-know facts are modest in number and complexity.

submersible pumps

Every tabletop fountain needs a submersible pump to circulate water. These pumps, first used in fish aquariums, are widely available at a reasonable cost. Submersible pumps are remarkably small, usually no larger than 2 x 1½ x 2¼ inches (5 x 3.8 x 5.7 cm), allowing them to fit easily into almost any container. A pump is run by a magnetic impeller motor secured within a waterproof epoxy case. This is a significant technological advancement over earlier models. The modern epoxy case blocks water from leaking into the motor and causing damage. The submersible pump's motor draws standing water through an intake filter and pushes it up and out a spout. To accomplish this the pump's motor must have an energy source. Electricity powers most pump motors, though solar and battery-operated models do exist. You can purchase submersible pumps at many retailers, including larger craft stores, garden outlets, and aquarium suppliers. The plastic tubing that you'll need to direct water flow is sold separately. If you have difficulty locating a submersible pump in your area, many companies offer fountain pumps online, or by phone and catalogue order.

tips on choosing the right pump

Before buying a pump for your project, consider its mechanical capabilities in relation to your design. Pumps with water flow regulators let you choose from multiple pressure settings. This gives you added control over the water, allowing you to fine-tune your fountain's performance. A pump with a water flow regulator will also work in a wider range of fountain designs. You can transfer the same pump from a quiet fountain with a low, oozing trickle to a tall fountain with a gushing spray. When setting up your fountain, always adjust the pump to its lowest setting. Gradually raise the water flow to the desired level.

Disassembled fountain pump

Another factor to consider is the maximum lift of the pump. Submersible pumps are classified by a measurement of volume. The recognized standard is GPH (gallons per hour) or LPH (liters per hour). Most tabletop fountains run from 25 to a maximum of 80 GPH (100 to 300 L per hour). This is the maximum volume of water the pump circulates without attachments, such as plastic tubing, on its output valve, or spout. With the addition of tubing, the height of the water flow increases, but the pump's GPH or LPH decreases. Submersible pumps can only lift water to a certain height before they run out of power. This measurement, often called *max head*, is printed by the manufacturer on the pump's packaging or enclosed on its spec sheet.

Submersible fountain pump

Knowing where you plan to display your completed fountain can also help you pick the right pump. If you choose a pump that runs on electricity, you'll need to plug the cord into an outlet. Measure the distance from your fountain's ideal location to the nearest outlet, and note the length of cord needed to run from the pump to the wall. A short 12-inch (30.5 cm) pump cord limits where your fountain can be displayed. A 3- to 5-foot (.9 to 1.5 m) pump cord gives you more options for fountain placement, but also more cord to conceal from view. If you use an extension cord, make sure it's the correct type to safely conduct the power from the pump cord to the wall outlet. Some pumps come with a power switch located on their cord. This convenient option provides easier access for starting and stopping your fountain. You can purchase a power switch and install it onto your pump cord at home. Make sure to follow the switch manufacturer's instructions completely.

If you've already selected a fountain container, its depth could factor into choosing the right submersible pump. The pump's intake filter must always remain below water at a depth recommended by the pump manufacturer. The location of a submersible pump's intake filter varies. A pump with an intake filter on its bottom edge can operate in less water, making it suitable for a more shallow fountain container. Pumps with a side or top edge intake filter require deeper water and deeper containers. It's most often advised to have at least $1\frac{1}{2}$ inches (3.8 cm) of water covering the intake filter, but always consult your pump's operating instructions for individual pump standards.

other pump variables

Submersible pump motors differ in noise level. Some emit a virtually silent hum; others, a distinct and constant churning. Select a pump you can live with.

In most fountain designs you'll want to conceal the pump. A smaller pump is easier to disguise.

Submersible pumps are usually designed to expel water through a spout on their top surface. This configuration suits the majority of designs. If, however, you want water to come out from the side of a pump, look for a model with a side outtake. Alternately, you can place a top-spout pump on its side if you make two simple design modifications: adjust the water level in the container to cover a higher intake valve, and devise some way to secure the pump in place.

Submersible pumps require little maintenance. A regular cleaning to remove accumulated scum, dirt, or debris is generally sufficient. Consult the pump owner's manual for specific maintenance instructions, and choose a pump consistent with the amount of care you're willing to give.

Make sure the voltage of the pump matches the voltage of your electrical outlets. North America and the majority of South America use a 120 volt pump. Europe uses a 230 or 240 volt pump. If you live in Australia, the European pump works, as long as you install an adapter onto the plug.

A variety of fountain containers

containers

Now you're ready to express yourself creatively. The first step is to find a container that complements your decor, shows your spirit, or has unique character. Searching for and selecting a container for your tabletop fountain project can be very entertaining. Unique vessels can be found in many places, from ritzy home stores to weekend flea markets. You might even have a great fountain container tucked away in some dark corner of your attic. Once you've made a few tabletop fountains, you'll begin to see potential fountain containers everywhere!

A fountain container's ultimate success relies both on its looks and its ability to perform a few important roles. Most critically, a fountain container

bowl. Many common fountain accents, such as slate and stone, are quite heavy and need a reliable container.

tips on choosing the right container

Look for reservoirs that are receptive to further embellishment. Wide-rimmed or terra-cotta bowls are ideal for mosaic. Glass containers are a delight to paint or etch with specialty products. Remember that the pump cord has to exit the container at some point. Select a container that's easy to drill, cut, or grind, if you wish to notch its rim to camouflage the cord. Be sure the container fits your location; if the rim of the vessel hangs over the edge of your display surface, the fountain is more likely to be bumped, causing spills or damage. One last factor: consider your commitment to maintaining your fountain; you'll have to add water more frequently to a shallow reservoir.

waterproofing containers

Once you select a container, fill it with water and let it sit for 24 hours. Obvious leakage can be observed immediately, while subtle seeping may take more time to discover. Note the water level when you first fill your bowl. If you notice any change after 24 hours, reinforce the container with a water sealant. For minor problems, such as loose seams, apply a line of silicone caulk to quickly and easily seal the joint. Topcoat the caulk with several layers of waterproofing varnish or sealant to finish the job. If your reservoir has major problems holding water, the simplest solution is to find a plastic bowl or sturdy liner to fit inside the container.

must hold water. For many typical containers, such as those made from glazed ceramic, seamless metal, glass, resin, or plastic, this is a natural ability. If a non-traditional container strikes your fancy, but doesn't hold water, don't fret. There are many solutions for making a fountain container waterproof (see page 15 for several ideas). Once you know your container will hold water, you must determine if it holds enough water to run the submersible pump. Refer to the pump manufacturer's specifications to see how much water is required, and make sure the container accommodates this depth. Lastly, a fountain container should be sturdy with a level base. It has to support the pump, the water, and any other elements added to the

container	recommended sealant
ceramic	silicone caulk, concrete waterproofing solution
clay	terra-cotta sealant in spray or liquid, concrete and masonry sealant, spray or liquid polyurethene, acrylic sealants in spray or liquid form
metal	silicone caulk for kitchen or bath, aquarium sealant, underwater epoxy, epoxy putty
slate	concrete sealant, polyurethene
stone	polyurethene
wood	secure plastic liner or interior container

Different waterproofing methods and products are used to seal different materials. The chart above is a good starting point for waterproofing options. Bring your container to a local hardware store and ask for a salesperson's help, if you still aren't sure which product to use.

water

Water straight from the tap in your house is fine to use in your tabletop fountain as long as it isn't too hard. Bottled water can also be used but is probably not worth the expense. Some bottled waters may actually speed the growth of algae and other unwanted organisms. Keep the water temperature in your fountain between 32° and 98°F (0° and 37°C). A drop in water temperature below the freezing point burns out the pump's motor. Your tabletop fountain recirculates most of its water supply. A conspicuous loss of water from the container is most often caused by rapid evaporation or oversplash. Fountains in an arid environment need more frequent refilling. Avoid oversplash by adding or

rearranging fountain accents, decreasing pump pressure, increasing the diameter of the plastic tubing, or selecting a larger container. A tabletop fountain is a great humidifier, especially in dry climates. It adds much-needed moisture to the air for people, plants, and animals. With this in mind, make sure that any chemical additives placed in the water are safe for all living things.

If you're feeling wild go ahead and add a little food coloring to the water (see the Avalon Ice Fountain on page 71). Change the color of the water as often as you like to reflect the season, create a mood, or correspond to an interior design scheme. Proceed with caution, however, if you intend to replace the water in your fountain with other liquids such as champagne or bubble bath. Test the pH of the alternate substance first to make sure it complies with the specifications of your pump. Consult the manufacturer's operating information to find the acceptable range of pH.

electricity

It's a common fear that the use of electricity in or around water is dangerous. It can be, but rest assured that your fountain pumps are totally sealed for your protection. Some electrical appliances in your home, such as hair-dryers and toasters, are typically used near a water supply and should be handled with caution in this environment. A submersible fountain pump, however, is designed to go in the water. Its contact with water is no accident. Ease any lingering concerns about safety by using a GFCI outlet or adapter (see page 23 for more information).

Plastic tubing, various diameters

tubing

Attaching plastic tubing around the pump spout lets you lift and direct the water. For optimum performance, you should have a tight seal between the spout and the tube. Luckily, the flexibility of the plastic and the length of the spout work together to make this connection smooth and effortless.

The flexible clear plastic tubing used for tabletop fountains is a common variety stocked at any hardware store. Look in the plumbing department and you'll find an ample supply of inexpensive tubing. You can also find tubing supplies at gardening, pet, and craft retailers. Your pump's operating instructions may not specify what size tubing to purchase. Not to worry—just bring your pump with you and test different tubes to find the right fit.

Once you bring your flexible plastic tubing home, trim it to size with sharp scissors, or a craft or utility knife. Precut lengths of tubing are frequently sold wrapped in a coil, so curved tubing is a common problem. Straighten curved tubing by dipping it in very hot water, then slipping it over a piece of wooden dowel.

Improve your fountain building skills by knowing how plastic tubing is sized and using that knowledge to your advantage. Plastic tubing's outside diameter, or *OD*, is the diameter of the exterior tube walls. Its inside diameter, or *ID*, is the diameter of the interior tube walls. The wall thickness of plastic tubing is $\frac{1}{16}$ inch (1.6 mm), so the difference between a tube's outside and inside diameters is $\frac{1}{8}$ inch (3 mm). Tubing is sold in $\frac{1}{8}$ inch (3 mm) increments of the inside diameter so that different sizes can be telescoped. To telescope tubing means to gradually increase or decrease the diameter of pieces as you put them together. This practice lets you build additional water pressure (narrow tubing exerts a greater force on the water, causing a higher flow), direct the flow of the water with greater precision, and match the diameter of your spout to the mouth of your fountain.

Telescoped plastic tubing

Specialty adapters, such as "Y" and "T" attachments (named for their shapes), fit onto plastic tubing. They're used to split water flow into two streams. Remember to increase your pump's water flow regulator setting to provide enough pressure for both streams.

supports

Sound construction leads to a long and trouble-free life for your tabletop fountain. A good fountain design protects its components from excess weight, minimizes the chance of debris blockage, and facilitates steady water circulation. Though mostly hidden from view, fountain supports play a very important role.

collars

A collar is a fountain pump's bodyguard, surrounding it, protecting it from hazard, and concealing it from view. Collars sit flat on the base of the container, and must be made from a waterproof material. At least three notches are cut at the bottom of every collar. The pump cord passes under one notch, and the other notches help with water circulation. If the collar encases the pump completely, it must also have a hole at the top for the spout's tubing. A collar shields a pump from contact with fountain filler, such as rocks and pebbles. This helps reduce noise by eliminating contact vibrations. It also limits the potential for clogged filters and motor damage.

Weight-bearing collars must equal or surpass the height of the pump to be effective. They provide a sturdy foundation for heavy fountains without putting any pressure on the pump. Use non-weight-bearing collars only when a fountain design has no load on the pump. Under this circumstance, the collar only has to be tall enough to guard the pump's intake filter from debris.

Left to right: tray, fountain head on collar, collar

Pre-fabricated collars can be purchased where tabletop fountain supplies are sold. If you choose to buy a collar, make sure its height is appropriate for the depth of your container and your overall fountain design. Creating your own fountain collar is inexpensive and simple. Select a material that's waterproof and sturdy, yet easy to cut, grind, or drill for notches. Plumbing couplings, PVC pipes, terracotta pots, even rigid plastic food containers, all make excellent fountain collars. Non-weight-bearing collars can be as modest as a trimmed plastic cup or soda bottle.

harnessing the benefits of negative ions

In spite of the "negative" connotation, negative air ions are very positive things! It's thanks to them that sitting near a waterfall, seashore, or your handcrafted fountain doesn't just *seem* physically and emotionally rejuvenating—it really is!

Any atom or molecule that gains an electron attains a negative charge. It's then a negative ion. The exchange of electrons is constant, but you'd need an electron microscope to see it. Negative air ions are created naturally by lightning, a pounding ocean surf, and waterfalls. Notice how the last two methods employ moving water? That means your fountain will create negative air ions, too.

Considerable research conducted over the past 20 years reveals that exposure to negative air ions benefits people in an extraordinary range of ways. The particles ease the symptoms of illnesses that have a physical origin, including SAD (seasonal affective disorder), hay fever, and asthma. These invisible benefactors help alleviate depression, irritability, insomnia, and tension—ailments which can have a psychological basis but typically impair physical health as well. Negative ions are also credited with reducing blood pressure, improving metabolism, and boosting the ability of the central nervous system to cope with the stress of everyday environmental hazards.

This means the most rewarding souvenir from a wilderness hike or trip to the beach might be better health. And that better health could be right around the corner—your tabletop fountain!

Here's where you can find negative ions, and how many you'll encounter (on average) per cubic centimeter:

Sealed steel-structure office building, with central heating and air conditioning: 0-250
Smoky indoor air: 0-100
Inside an airplane: 20-250
Normal indoor air (windows open): 250-500
Urban air in average industrial city: 250-750
Mountain air: 1,000-5,000
Country air: 1,000-20,100
Inside caves: 5,000-20,000
Beside waterfalls: 25,000-100,000

did you know?

trays

Trays provide a stiff, flat surface for fountain filler above the pump. The tray supports the weight of additional fountain elements. The collar may or may not support the weight of the tray. Using a tray means you'll need less filler material for your fountain. This saves money and produces a significantly lighter fountain. Using a tray also keeps more water in the base of the container so you can water your fountain less frequently.

rigid tubing

Certain fountain designs may put too much pressure on the thin plastic tubing, which can crimp or fold under the weight of heavy fountain elements. Give your tubing extra support by feeding it through a piece of rigid pipe. Plastic, copper, aluminum, or steel pipe, or even a piece of dried bamboo, can be sized to fit and slipped over the plastic tube to protect it.

glues

You'll often want to secure fountain elements in place. Use epoxy or silicone specialty glues on almost any surface to achieve a waterproof, clear, and lasting bond. Remember that you'll eventually have to access the pump for cleaning. Affix your fountain elements so they won't interfere with routine maintenance.

19

fountain heads

When water flows out of a specific fountain element, that structure is called the fountain head. Fountain heads are higher than the pump, and may or may not be attached to a collar or tray. Panda Paradise on page 102 and Slate Obelisk on page 106 feature particularly well-defined fountain heads.

fillers

Handsome river stones or tumbled shards of glass displayed in a tabletop fountain are most often noted for their elegant appearance, but their contribution is greater than just looks. Part of the creativity of fountain building is concocting ways to hide the pump. This is a terrific job for filler. Filler material can also guide the flow of the water, reduce splash, and refine a fountain's acoustics. Some of the most common (and beautiful) fountain fillers are stones, slate, gems, shells, sea glass, and marbles. These objects not only have a unique appearance—they're also naturally waterproof.

collectibles

Shells found on a beach vacation or rocks from your own backyard often have special meaning. A fantastic tabletop fountain is one of the best ways to give these treasures a lasting place in the spotlight. You can also display new specimens of gems and minerals in your fountain. Whether you collect rocks outdoors or through gem shows and retailers, you'll always have something fascinating to exhibit.

tumbled shards

To make your own glass shards from bottles or jars, you'll need an old bath towel, newspaper, a hammer, safety goggles, and a sturdy pair of work gloves. Cover a strong, level work surface with newspapers. Fold the towel into a multilayered square and place it on top of the newspaper. Center your glass object between the layers of the towel. Put on your safety goggles and gloves. With one hand, hold down the seams of the folded towel. Use the other hand to hammer the towel-wrapped glass object. Lift back one corner of the towel to see the results. If your shards are too large, repeat this process until you're satisfied with the result, or use tile nippers to trim any shard down to size.

lapidary tumbler

A lapidary (or rock) tumbler has a rotating barrel that simulates the action of waves. By using a more abrasive grit (silicon carbide) than sand and by maintaining a constant speed of rotation, tumblers produce artificial beach glass in a fraction of the time nature does. Shards of glass placed in the tumbler are continually cascaded down its walls and through a coarse abrasive slurry. The desired matte finish and rounded blunt shape is achieved after six to eight hours, a short time in the lapidary world. Only a hobby-quality rock tumbler is needed to work with glass, although more expensive varieties are available.

did you know?

rocks and glass

Tumbling rocks and glass is a hobby that's very compatible with creating tabletop fountains. With a texture similar to beach glass worn by the rolling ocean tides, tumbled glass is now commercially available in most craft stores. Look in the glass crafts department first, but you may also find pre-tumbled shards amongst the floral supplies. Tumbled glass is also available wherever aquarium supplies are sold. If you can't find a specific color or shape, you're not out of luck. The high-gloss finish of any small glass surface, such as a marble, jewel, or bottle shard, can be worn away to a frosted finish simply and easily with a rock tumbler. See page 20 to find out how to create your own. Glass half-marbles are popular embellishments that come in many colors, shapes, and sizes. They range in clarity from transparent to opaque, and some even project an iridescent glow. Ordinary half-marbles can be super stylish. Try tumbling, etching, or painting them for a unique look.

special effects

The technological achievement of small and affordable underwater lights and foggers adds a new dimension to contemporary fountain designs. You can now dramatically illuminate fountain elements with clear or colored halogen spotlights. These waterproof bulbs must stay submerged while in use, as the temperature of the surrounding water keeps the bulb cool. The oils on your hands can damage new bulbs, so cover them with a piece of tissue paper before handling. Fountain foggers, also called misters, are ultrasonic vaporizers. They produce a cloud of steam 12 inches (30.5 cm) in diameter and approximately 4 to 5 inches (10.2 to 12.7 cm) high. Fountain foggers dissipate about 1 quart (.95 L) of water in 4 to 5 hours, and will automatically shut off when the water level becomes too low. These units are for use in indoor fountains only.

drilling

You can create lovely fountains without drilling a single hole. Smart shopping can lead you to fountain elements that are either pre-drilled or have serendipitous hole placement. However, if you want or need to drill, here's a beginner's guide.

Drills that have variable speed settings are compatible with a wider variety of materials. Some surfaces, such as metal, need slow steady pressure while others, such as ceramics, are more receptive to high velocity. Variable speed drills give you the most control over your work and produce better results.

Drill bits differ in shape depending upon the surface they're intended to penetrate. There are different drill bits for masonry, wood, and metal. Make sure to purchase and install the correct bit into your drill before beginning a project. For fountain projects, you'll most often want to use a drill bit that's the same diameter as your plastic tubing. Not all drill attachments are intended to bore holes. Grinding, shaping, and polishing wheels are very useful installed on a drill.

If you're a beginner, practice drilling on a surface similar to your fountain element. Start your drill on the lowest speed. When you're comfortable with the slow action, increase the speed of the drill until you make a hole. The most prudent way to drill is to make a small pilot hole, then gradually increase the diameter of the bit until you reach the desired size. At some point, you're likely to break or crack an object while drilling. If the object isn't meant to hold water, you can repair it with epoxy or silicone caulk. Some cracks don't even have to be fixed, just strategically positioned out of sight.

safety, please

Always wear safety goggles when you're using a drill, as tiny flying particles of stone, masonry, or metal can harm your eyes. Working in sturdy gloves helps you maintain a firm grip on the object as you drill. Gloves also protect your hands from irritating splinters, but more importantly, from a sharp runaway revolving bit. A dust mask is essential to bar dust and grit from entering your lungs. Use a vise clamp whenever possible to lock an object in place while you drill. You'll control the drill better with two hands free.

Drilled hole in slate

ground fault circuit interrupters

An unintentional electric path between a source of current and a grounded surface is a *ground fault*. Ground faults occur when current is leaking somewhere; in effect, electricity is escaping to the ground.

A ground fault circuit interrupter (GFCI) protects you from electric shock by interrupting the flow of electrical current. Normally, electrical current is equal in the hot and neutral lines of a circuit. A GFCI monitors these currents. If this highly sensitive device detects a difference between the hot and neutral line it will trip the circuit within a fraction of a second to protect you.

GFCI outlets usually have a test and a reset button. The test button intentionally deactivates the outlet to insure proper function. The reset button returns your outlet to normal after a test or a fault. If you have a GFCI that has tripped and won't reset, you may have a wiring short in the circuit, a defective appliance on the circuit, or the GFCI itself may be defective.

Three types of GFCI outlets are available for home use. Permanent GFCIs can be installed as wall outlets or in circuit breaker boxes. Portable GFCIs can be used wherever permanent installations are not practical. A box containing the GFCI circuitry plugs into a standard outlet and the electrical product plugs into the box. Always perform a safety test on your portable GFCI each time before using it. Push the test button, which should kill power to the outlets. Then, press the reset button to restore power to the GFCI outlets. Retest the GFCI outlet once a month to make sure it is working properly. The portable GFCI requires no special knowledge or equipment to install.

did you know?

design ideas

You can learn a lot by observing how different tabletop fountains are put together. As a beginning fountain maker, you'll need to understand basic building ideas and how fountain parts are assembled and hidden. These diagrams reveal both simple and unusual camouflaging methods. Use them as teaching tools to test and expand your knowlege of fountain construction.

Indigo Inspiration
page 32

Designer: Marthe Le Van

This fountain proves that anything that's waterproof and catches your eye can be a fountain element. The submersible pump is resting on the base of the pedestal bowl. A non-weight-bearing white plastic collar surrounds the pump to camouflage its dark color. Clear plastic tubing is attached to the pump spout. A frosted glass fountain head fits over the pump and the collar. The tubing is fed through the hole in the fountain head and trimmed flush. Clear glass paperweights, a pillar candle tray, and tea light candleholders are added to completely conceal the mechanics.

Harmony Fountain
page 56

Designer: Tony Estrada

Copper pipes are visually appealing and offer rigid support for plastic tubing. In this fountain, the submersible pump rests on the bottom of the bowl. The pump is surrounded by a sturdy, weight-bearing collar. A piece of carved and drilled slate sits on top of the collar to hide the pump. A long piece of clear plastic tubing is connected to the pump spout and fed up the longest length of copper pipe.

Seashore Memory Fountain
page 68

Designer: Paris Mannion

This great "collector's fountain" provides plenty of room to showcase treasured beach finds. Ingeniously, these elements become critical to disguising its mechanics. The top of the pump is hidden by a slate lid while the sides of the pump are surrounded by loose decorative materials. The slate and spiral shell are both drilled to accommodate the flexible plastic tubing. The tubing is connected to the pump's spout and directs the fountain water upward to flow out of the shell.

25

Bamboo Fountain
page 74

Designer: Tony Estrada

Bamboo is an aethetically pleasing and practical choice to support plastic tubing. In this design, the submersible pump rests on the bottom of the bowl. The pump is surrounded by a sturdy, weight-bearing collar. A piece of carved and drilled slate sits on top of the collar to hide the pump. A long piece of clear plastic tubing is connected to the pump spout, fed up the vertical length of bamboo, and through a hole drilled in the bottom edge of the horizonal bamboo.

Love Eternal Fountain
page 86

Designer: Todd Browning

The lovely gems and stones featured here are not only decorative but also strategically mounted on top of PVC pipes to hide the fountain pump and tubing. The submersible pump rests on the base of the bowl. A length of plastic tubing is attached to the pump spout at one end. The other end of the tube is fed through a hole in the second layer of stone.

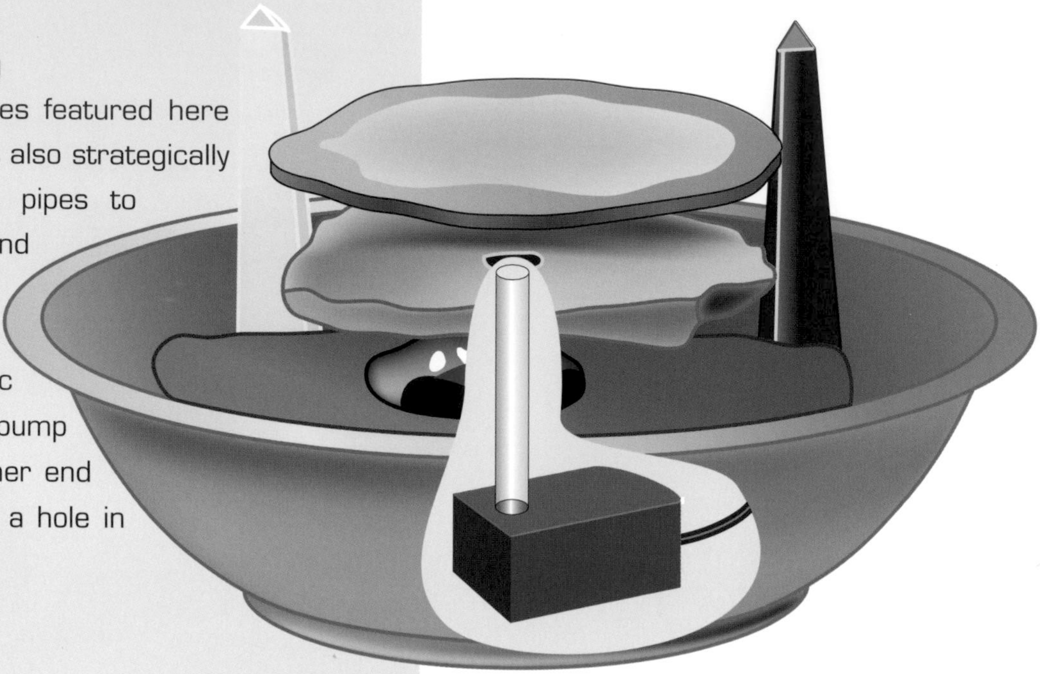

26

Panda Paradise
page 102

Designer: Nancy Carr

This fountain design effectively disguises all its inner-workings with permanent elements. The fountain pump sits flat on the bottom of the basin, and is surrounded by a sturdy weight-bearing collar. A stone wall fits around, but isn't attached to, the collar. To form the fountain head, plastic tubing is fed through a stack of drilled slate and epoxied. The fountain head is attached to the top edge of the collar.

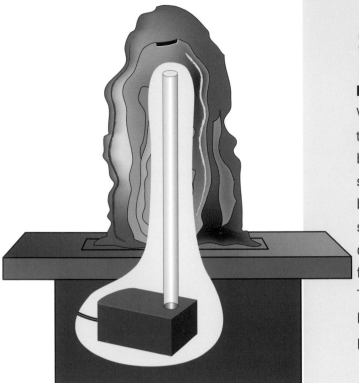

Slate Obelisk
page 106

Designer: Tony Estrada

With so little of its workings exposed, you'd think that this fountain was terribly complex, but closer examination proves just the opposite. The submersible pump sits flat on the base of the slate box. It's surrounded by a sturdy, weight-bearing collar. The slate obelisk fountain head is constructed with the flexible plastic tubing running down its length. There's enough excess plastic tubing at the base of the fountain head to connect to the pump's spout.

Copper Washboard Fountain, page 112

Designer: Tony Estrada

This design has a definite front and back side. The tubing is exposed in the back but hidden from view by the copper washboard. The submersible pump rests on the bottom of the bowl. The pump is surrounded by a sturdy, weight-bearing collar. A piece of carved and drilled slate sits on top of the collar to hide the pump. A short length of clear plastic tubing connects the pump's spout to a piece of copper pipe.

troubleshooting

Each fountain presents new challenges. One of the many joys of fountain building is problem-solving. When an obstacle presents itself, there's hardly anything more satisfying than realizing its solution. The conditions described below are routine fountain difficulties with easy remedies.

noises

All pump motors hum. Excessive pump noise can originate in several places. If your pump makes unusual gasping, grumbling, or sucking noises, it's probably in need of water. Check the level in your container. A water level below the intake filter causes a submersible pump to draw air. This puts stress on the motor and may cause it to stop working. Check for debris blocking the pump's intake valve and remove any obstructions. If your pump has suction cup feet, make sure they're firmly suctioned to the base of the container.

Look at the inner arrangement of the fountain parts. A pump that touches the side of a collar or other support structure can generate surplus noise. Fountain filler, such as stones and marbles, can also rattle against the pump. Move the pump to the center of the collar away from its walls. Permanently position the fountain filler away from the pump. Adjust the fountain's water flow by raising or lowering the pump pressure, or changing the course of the stream.

Examine the location of your fountain. It may be resting on a surface that actually amplifies the sound of the running motor. If you don't want to move your fountain, place it on top of foam or a mat.

water

If the water in your fountain appears dirty or hazy, turn the pump off and disassemble the fountain. Clean the container and the pump, especially the impeller and water intake filter. Reconstruct the fountain and add fresh water. Keep tabletop fountains out of direct sunlight to slow algae growth.

pump

If the pump isn't working, make sure it's plugged into a properly functioning outlet. Check that the pump's water flow regulator isn't turned completely down or off, and that nothing is stuck in the pump's impeller.

bamboo techniques

cleaning

Bamboo can have surface dirt and mildew. To regain luster and shine, wash bamboo thoroughly with soap and water. Remove mold and fungus by rubbing the affected areas with a cloth moistened with isopropyl alcohol. Alcohol ends the life of mold or fungus organisms, sterilizes the bamboo, and disappears from its surface quickly and completely.

cutting and drilling

You'll need a saw with a sharp blade to cut directly across a *culm*, or bamboo stem. Many saws, such as handsaws for tree pruning, will work for rough cuts. Use a pull saw with a thin blade and 22 teeth per inch (2.5 cm) for fine cuts. Good results can also be obtained from hacksaws designed for cutting metal, heavily-weighted Japanese saws with special blades for bamboo, power saws, and the fine teeth of a ceramic disc blade.

Guide your saw with a miter box to make an angled cut. Mark the desired angle on the bamboo, and place it in the miter box. Align the mark with the proper set of slots, secure the bamboo, and saw.

Although bamboo is primarily hollow, it's completely sealed at each joint. For plastic tubing to pass through bamboo, drill through its interior walls with a wood bit.

smoothing and polishing

Cut bamboo is sharp, and bamboo splinters are painful, so wear sturdy work gloves. A beveled knife or shaver can smooth the slivered edges of the inner wall. Smooth drilled edges with a curved or round rasp. Achieve the most polished appearance on cut and smoothed bamboo edges by using a sanding sponge—your bamboo will look and feel like silk.

Use fine-grade steel wool to shine up a dull culm and to remove the chalky-white deposit found on the surface of some bamboos. Dip the steel wool in water, rub the pad up and down, and work in sections until a lustrous appearance is achieved.

staining and sealing

Subjected to the elements, bamboo's surface layer eventually wears down and becomes irregular. A roughened bamboo surface can be a blessing in disguise. In this condition, bamboo will accept finishes which otherwise wouldn't adhere to its waxy silicone surface.

Stains give bamboo new life. Wash all dirt and mildew from cured and weathered bamboo, and let dry. Rub the stain onto the bamboo with a soft cloth. Since the stain clings to the bamboo's surface rather than permeating it, a second coat may be required. Outdoor projects that have become pitted should be protected with a sealant. For indoor bamboo elements, tung oil, camellia oil, and floor wax are good sealers.

did you know?

projects

Designer: Marthe Le Van

Tiny Fountain

This fountain is small enough to fit on a window ledge or nightstand, and it's incredibly simple to assemble. Choose a shallow, single-colored bonsai dish to complement a multi-colored glazed ceramic bowl, and you've got a completely original designer accent.

What You Need

Small shallow bonsai dish or ceramic bowl, 2 x 4 inches (5 x 10.2 cm)

Variable speed drill, optional

Masonry drill bit, larger diameter than pump spout, optional

Safety goggles and dust mask, if drilling

Ceramic bowl, 4 x 5 inches (10.2 x 12.7 cm)

Submersible pump

Decorative rocks

1 If the small shallow bowl you've selected doesn't have a pre-drilled hole, measure and mark its center point on the bottom. Wearing safety goggles and a dust mask, use the masonry bit to drill a hole through the mark. Clean off the ceramic dust with a damp sponge or rag.

2 Adjust the pump's water flow regulator to its lowest setting. Position the pump on the base of the deeper ceramic bowl. The pump spout should be off-center, much closer to one wall of the bowl. Limited interior space in this bowl prevents the use of a collar, and its minimal height makes plastic tubing dispensable.

3 Place the hole in the base of the bonsai dish or drilled shallow bowl over the pump spout. Angle the dish or bowl to rest on both the pump spout and the interior wall of the deeper bowl.

4 Pour enough water into the deeper ceramic container to cover the pump's intake valve. Fill the bonsai dish or shallow bowl with the decorative rocks. Arrange an attractive display that appeals to the eye and disguises the pump spout and hole.

5 Turn on the pump and observe the flow of the water. Fine-tune the placement of the rocks for visual and acoustic appeal. Adjust the pump's water flow regulator to a higher setting if needed.

Sake Fountain

If you're seeking simplicity, look no further than this graceful fountain. Its soft flowing lines guide the water on a peaceful passage, and its acoustics are positively intoxicating. All the fountain elements were cleverly adapted from their original function and show the true innovative quality of fountain making.

What You Need

Square ceramic vessel with sloping sides, $4^1/_2$ x 7 x 7 inches (11.4 x 17.8 x 17.8 cm)

Square tile, $5\,^3/_4$ x $5\,^3/_4$ x $^1/_4$ inches (14.6 x 14.6 x .6 cm)

Safety goggles

Dust mask

Variable speed drill

Masonry drill bit, same diameter as plastic tubing

Ceramic sake bottle, 7 inches (17.8 cm) high, $2\,^3/_4$-inch (7 cm) diameter base, $^3/_4$-inch (1.9 cm) diameter rim

Submersible pump

Clear plastic tubing, to fit over pump spout

Collar, 4 to $4^1/_2$ inches (10.2 to 11.4 cm) high, with 3 notches for pump cord and water circulation

Sake cup, optional

1. Select a tile that fits snugly under the rim of the ceramic vessel. You may have to angle the tile to wedge it into the vessel. If you choose a tile that's too large you can have it custom cut at a tile center to fit your vessel.

2. Measure and mark the center point on the face of the tile. Wearing safety goggles and a dust mask, use the masonry bit to drill a hole at this point. Clean the dust off the tile.

3. Measure and mark the center point on the bottom of the ceramic bottle. Wearing safety goggles and a dust mask, use the masonry bit to drill a hole at this point. Clean the dust off the bottle.

4. Adjust the pump's water flow regulator to its lowest setting. Slide the clear plastic tubing over the pump's spout, making a secure connection. Position the pump and collar on the base of the ceramic vessel. Add enough water to the vessel to cover the pump's intake valve. Feed the plastic tube through the hole in the square tile and slide the tile

feng shui

Did you know that having an indoor fountain can boost your career? Practitioners of feng shui believe that the judicious placement of buildings, and everything in them, causes harmony with the energy of the surrounding environment, resulting in an improved life.

The words feng shui (pronounced "feng shwa," "fung shui," or "fung shuway," depending whether you are Mandarin, Cantonese, or American) mean "wind and water." Traditionally taught and practiced in the Far East, feng shui originated as a method for finding proper sites for graves, and gradually came to encompass the home.

This wisdom was not only understood and practiced in the Orient; all parts of the world have drawn on traditional ideas for the design and position of homes and places of worship. In Europe, pre-historic, medieval, and more modern structures have been built in a certain fashion and on certain sites for a specific purpose.

According to feng shui, areas in the home (or office) relate to certain spheres of human life, such as wisdom, creativity, and relationships. The point of feng shui is to keep energy, called *chi*, flowing through your environment. If certain sectors of the house have negative space, you can counteract that by stimulating the chi through your furnishings and object placement. Feng shui can also focus the type of energy you want to maintain in your life.

Tall, upright plants have a strong, upward energy that counteracts the draining of energy. Place cleansing plants next to electrical units, such as the pump cord and wall socket, to counteract debilitating electro-magnetic discharges.

In feng shui, water represents the journey through life, as well as the career. Still water causes stagnation. Therefore, a bubbling fountain in the home will help keep your career moving forward and your life running smoothly.

down the tube until it sits flat on the collar. Angle the tile if necessary to fit it in the vessel. You may have to crop the top of the collar to fit the tile in the vessel.

5 Trim the plastic tubing to approximately 1 inch (2.5 cm) below the rim of the bottle. Feed the tubing through the hole in the bottom of the sake bottle. Slide the bottle down the tube until it sits flat on the tile. Turn on the pump. Water will fill the sake bottle, overflow down its sides, and travel across the tile back into the vessel. If desired, place a sake cup on the tile for a decorative touch.

did you know?

Copper Jet Fountain

This fountain's rivulets of water flow from well-placed holes in a
central capped copper pipe. Rainbow rocks mix with brick chips to
create a palette of desert colors that intensify the warmth of the copper.

What You Need

*Capped copper pipe, 8 inches (20.3 cm) long, ⅝ inch (1.6 cm) in diameter

1-inch-wide (2.5 cm) masking tape

Vise clamp, or two wooden dowels

Awl and hammer, or variable speed drill with ⅛-inch (3 mm) metal drill bit

Clear plastic tubing, to fit pump spout

Pot with boiling water

Submersible pump

Round bowl, 3 x 14 inches (7.6 x 35.6 cm)

Rainbow rocks or other reddish-tan stones

*You can find capped copper pipe in the plumbing department at most hardware stores.

1 Adhere strips of masking tape vertically to the capped pipe, totally covering its copper surface. The tape makes the pipe easier to mark and drill.

2 Depending on the depth of your bowl, measure 3 to 3½ inches (7.6 to 8.9 cm) from the bottom of the pipe, and draw a ring around the pipe at this point. Draw a second ring ¾ inch (1.9 cm) above the first, and a third ring ¾ inch (1.9 cm) above the second.

3 Mark a large point on the bottom ring line to indicate the first hole. Mark a second point on the opposite side of the bottom ring line for the second hole.

4 Mark two large points on the middle ring line, opposite each other and centered between the points marked in Step 3. On the top ring line, mark two large points directly above the points marked in Step 3.

5 Clamp the capped pipe in the vise, or secure two wooden dowels on either side of the pipe with tape. Hammer the pointed awl into each large point, making a ⅛-inch (3 mm) hole. Alternately, wearing safety goggles, a dust mask, and work gloves, use the ⅛-inch (3 mm) metal bit to drill the holes. After making the holes, six in all, remove the masking tape from the pipe.

6 Submerge the plastic tubing into boiling water for 10 seconds. This softens and straightens the tubing so it can be compressed to fit into the copper pipe. Fit 2½ inches (6.4 cm) of straightened plastic tubing snugly into the copper pipe to help keep it upright.

7 Adjust the pump's water flow regulator to its lowest setting, and place the pump in the bowl with its spout at the center. Slide the bare tubing that extends from the copper pipe securely over the pump spout. Cut off excess tubing as needed for a close fit. Add enough water to the bowl to cover the pump intake valve, and plug in the pump cord.

8 Adjust the pump pressure as needed. Place the rainbow rocks or other reddish-tan stones on the perimeter of the bowl to deflect water and control splash. Add more rocks around the pump to stabilize the arrangement.

tip

If the spray from the jets is too powerful, there are several ways to bring it under control. You can enlarge the diameter of the middle ring of pipe holes, twist the copper pipe so the water lands on different rocks, or tilt the pipe slightly to change the angle of the jets. As a last resort, use a wider bowl.

maintenance

Keep the copper pipe bright and shiny by rubbing it with a quarter of a lemon sprinkled with salt. Left untreated, the pipe will naturally develop a lovely blue-green patina.

Designer: Marthe Le Van

Indigo Inspiration Fountain

This fountain's eclectic character gives it unlimited potential. It can be a focal point for personal contemplation one day and the centerpiece for a lavish party the next. The clear crystal balls reflect both the trickle of the water and the glow of the tea light candles to produce dazzling effects.

Submersible pump

Clear plastic tubing, to fit pump spout and fountain head

Glass pedestal bowl, 12 inches (30.5 cm) in diameter with a 4-inch-deep (10.2 cm) basin

*Glass fountain head

**8 round glass paperweights, 2½ inches (6.4 cm) in diameter

Flat glass candleholder with raised lip, 7½ inches (19 cm) in diameter

4 glass tea light candleholders

4 tea light candles

*A glass fountain head can be purchased where fountain supplies are sold, but you don't have to use glass. You can substitute your own version made from clear or frosted rigid plastic.

** These mass-produced paperweights were found at a discount store that sells overstock and close-out merchandise. The size and shape of these paperweights vary. Try to buy weights that are similar.

1 Adjust the pump's water flow regulator to its lowest setting. Slide the clear plastic tubing over the pump spout, making a secure connection. Position the pump on the base of the glass bowl with the spout in the center. Feed the tubing through the hole in the fountain head, and lower it onto the base of the bowl. Run the pump cord through the notch in the fountain head. Cut the tubing flush with the top of the fountain head's hole.

2 Evenly distribute seven glass paperweights around the circumference of the fountain head. Most round paperweights have one flat, unpolished side. Position this side against the fountain head to keep the weights from shifting.

3 Place the flat glass candleholder on top of the paperweights. Rest the candleholder on at least three balancing points for stability. If needed, adjust the paperweights under the glass until it sits level.

4 Fill the glass bowl with enough water to cover the pump's intake valve and turn on the pump. The water should pass through the tubing, rise to hit the underside of the glass candleholder, travel out along the flat glass to its edge, and fall back into the glass bowl. Make adjustments in pump pressure as needed.

5 Decorate the top of the candleholder with one centered paperweight flanked by four tea light holders. Place the tea lights into the holders on the top of the fountain, and light them for a special effect.

41

Bubbling Water Garden

A tabletop fountain makes a attractive home for low-maintenance water plants. This casual fountain design will look and sound sensational on a porch or deck where relaxation is your only concern.

What You Need

1-gallon (3.8 L) plastic milk container

Terra-cotta planter bowl, approximately 20 inches (50 cm) in diameter

Epoxy glue

Small plastic tub, for mixing the epoxy

Plastic knife

Silicone caulk

Water sealant

Spray paint (optional)

Semi-circular vinyl-coated wire grid shelf unit, found at home improvement centers

Potted bog plant, 4 inches (10 cm) tall (available at well-stocked garden centers)

Submersible pump

Bell fountainhead

River stones, polished river rocks, and shells

Water plants (as available at well-stocked garden centers)

1 Cut a flat 4-inch (10.2 cm) disk out of the plastic milk carton. Place it over the hole in the bottom of the planter. Apply the epoxy to the inside of the planter with the plastic knife to seal the disk edges and cover the hole. Weight down the disk until it's dry, approximately one hour.

2 Caulk the edges of the circle. Turn the planter over, and fill in the center hole with silicone caulk. Let the caulk set 24 hours.

3 Spray the interior of the planter with water sealant and let it dry. Apply a second coat and let it dry. If desired, spray paint the exterior of the planter.

4 Place the vinyl shelf in the planter. Put the bog plant, still in its nursery pot, in the bottom of the planter. It may be necessary to cut ½ inch (1.3 cm) or so from the rim of the plant container so that it will just fit under the vinyl shelf. (Just be sure not to cut below the soil line!) If you would like the plant to sit higher in the arrangement, place it on a small rock.

43

5 Remove the shelf and the bog plant. Adjust the pump's water flow regulator to its lowest setting, and place it near the center of the planter. Set the vinyl shelf in the planter and position the bog plant at the open end. Attach the bell-spray fountain head attachment onto the pump through one of the square holes in the vinyl grid.

6 Add water almost to the top of the rim of the bog plant, making sure the pump's intake filter is covered. Arrange stones, rocks, and shells on the vinyl shelf, fully covering it. Arrange more water plants around the edges. Plug in the fountain, adjusting the bell spray nozzle and pump pressure until you get the sound you like. Make sure that the water does not splash over the edges.

Designer: Marthe Le Van

Peaceful Pagoda

This elegant fountain takes advantage of the unique shapes, graduated sizes, and ready-made holes of bonsai containers. Two rectangular, footed dishes stack to form the pagoda. Slate chips surround the structure to create a terrain, and fresh flowers and grasses adorn its rim.

2 ceramic bonsai containers, $2^{1}/_{2}$ x $4^{1}/_{4}$ x $3^{1}/_{2}$ inches (6.4 x 10.8 x 8.9 cm) and $2^{1}/_{2}$ x $5^{1}/_{4}$ x 4 inches (6.4 x 13.3 x 10.2 cm)

Safety goggles

Dust mask

Sturdy work gloves

Variable speed drill

Masonry drill bit, same diameter as plastic tubing, optional

*Square metal decorative container, 3 x $5^{1}/_{2}$ x $5^{1}/_{2}$ inches (7.6 x 14 x 14 cm)

Vise grip

Metal drill bit, same diameter as plastic tubing

Submersible pump

Clear plastic tubing, to fit the pump spout

Round ceramic bowl, $3^{1}/_{2}$ x 9 inches (8.9 x 22.9 cm)

Decorative rocks

Fresh flowers or grasses

* This metal box serves double duty as the pump's collar and as a decorative fountain element. Select a box that is small enough to fit within the diameter of the bowl but too large to rest flat on its base. Ideally, the four corners of the box balance on the bowl's interior walls, about one-third of the way to the top. The gap between the square box and the round bowl lets the pump cord exit the box. This important space also allows the fountain water to circulate.

1 If the bonsai containers you've selected don't have pre-drilled holes, measure and mark the center point on the bottom of both containers. Wearing the safety goggles, dust mask, and sturdy work gloves, use the masonry bit to drill a hole through the mark. Clean off the ceramic dust with a damp sponge or rag.

45

2 Measure and mark the center point on the underside of the metal box. Secure the box in the vise grip, and put on the safety goggles, dust mask, and sturdy work gloves. Using the metal bit, begin to drill on the lowest setting, applying more pressure and drill speed as required to penetrate the surface of, and eventually make a hole through the box. To prevent the bit from slipping, you may want to start by drilling a pilot hole with a smaller diameter bit. Once the correct size hole is drilled, remove the box from the vise grip. Carefully clean all metal shavings off the box, your work area, and gloves.

3 Adjust the pump's water flow regulator to its lowest setting. Place the clear plastic tubing over the pump spout and form a tight seal. Position the pump on the base of the bowl, with the spout at the center. Run the tubing through the hole in the center of the box, and slide the box down to perch on the sides of the ceramic bowl.

4 Feed the plastic tubing through the larger bonsai container from the bottom. Fill the container with the decorative rocks to surround the tube. Feed the remainder of the plastic tubing through the small bonsai container from the top. Guide the container down the tube to rest upside down on the rocks.

46

5 Cut the tube flush with the lip of the container. Place one thin narrow slate piece into the tubing to divert the water flow. Put two more pieces of slate on top of the roof of the pagoda. If the base of your metal box has a recessed surface, distribute slate on it also. Add fresh flowers or grass stems around the pagoda as desired.

6 Add enough water to the bowl to cover the pump's intake valve. Turn the pump on and observe the water flow. Adjust the rocks and the pump pressure for visual and acoustic appeal.

option

This is a very flexible fountain design. To form an open symmetrical structure, simply reverse the position of the small bonsai dish, then arrange rocks in the small bonsai container, surrounding and concealing the tube.

Designer: Todd Browning

Simple Spirit Fountain

With water rolling off layer after layer of exquisite stone, this
fountain is a hypnotizing blend of reflected light and soothing music.
Searching for the right rocks can be a rewarding adventure. Creating
the ambience for them to come to life as a fountain is, like most
projects, satisfying on both a technical and artistic level.

What You Need

PVC pipe, 1¹/₂ inches (3.8 cm) in diameter

Round bowl, 4 x 9 inches (10.2 x 22.9 cm)

3 blue agate slabs, small, medium (with hole), and large

Hacksaw or PVC cutter

Assorted seashells, small

Blue calcite

Waterproof epoxy

Clear acrylic rod, such as a window blind rod

Green tourmaline, 1 x ¹/₄ inch (2.5 x 3.2 cm)

Submersible pump

Clear plastic tubing, telescoped if needed to fit pump spout and agate hole

Green calcite, assorted pieces

Quartz point, rutilated

1 Measure, mark, and cut the PVC pipe to sit flat on the base of the bowl. Place the large agate slab on top of the pipe to test the fit. Adjust the height of the pipe as needed so the height of the agate slab equals the rim of the bowl.

2 Position one seashell (same thickness as the blue calcite) on the left front edge of the large agate slab. Place the blue calcite behind the shell. Adjust these elements as needed, then glue them in place with waterproof epoxy.

3 Measure from the base of the bowl to the top of the shell and calcite glued in Step 2. Mark and cut a piece of the clear acrylic rod to this measurement. Position the small blue agate slab on top of the seashell and blue calcite. Determine the location for the acrylic rod to support the left edge of the calcite slab. Adhere the clear acrylic rod to the base of the bowl with waterproof epoxy at this point.

4 Adhere the small blue agate slab on top of the seashell, blue calcite, and acrylic rod with waterproof epoxy. Make sure the seashell and calcite stick out from under the slab, and that the acrylic rod is hidden underneath.

5 Use waterproof epoxy to adhere the base of the green tourmaline to the right rear edge of the large blue agate slab. Arrange (but don't glue) the second seashell to the top center point on the small calcite slab. Place the medium agate slab on top of the second shell and tourmaline. If the agate isn't well-supported and level, select another shell. Once a suitable shell is found, glue it in place with epoxy.

6 Measure from the base of the bowl to the top of the tourmaline and second shell. Mark and cut a piece of the clear acrylic rod to this measurement. Place the medium calcite slab on top of the elements glued in Step 5. Determine the position for the cut acrylic rod, supporting the rear center edge of the agate slab. Use waterproof epoxy to adhere the rod to the base of the bowl at this location.

7 Place the medium blue agate slab on its three supports. Adjust its position to cover the tourmaline and the acrylic rod, but leave the seashell partially exposed. Glue the medium agate in place. Allow all epoxy to dry.

8 Adjust the pump's water flow regulator to its lowest setting. Slide the tubing over the pump spout and form a tight seal. Place the pump on the rear base of the bowl. Insert the pump's tubing into the agate's hole. If needed, remove the pump and trim its tubing in small increments for a solid and balanced fit. Fill the bowl with enough water to cover the pump's intake valve. Decorate the base of the bowl with green calcite, and turn on the fountain. Set the rutilated quartz point on the top agate near the fountain head to alter the flow of water, and increase the pump pressure as needed.

Designer: Tony Estrada

Earth Elements Fountain

A sensational slate piece set on a gentle slope is the basis of this elegant fountain design. Rock accents suggest a natural spring with water bubbling to the surface and rolling down the slate into an attractive copper container. A single flower bloom set into the slate gives a vivid dash of color, while two tea lights add a glowing warmth.

What You Need

- Slate tile, as wide as bowl, at least 1 1/2 to 2 inches (3.8 to 5 cm) thick
- Safety goggles
- Dust mask
- Work gloves
- Small diamond grinding wheel
- Variable speed drill
- Small motorized rotary tool, optional
- 4-inch (10.2 cm) grinder with masonry grinding wheel, optional
- Masonry drill bit, same diameter as plastic tubing
- Carbide grit hole saw, 1 1/2 inches (3.8 cm) or similar size
- Hammer
- 1-inch (2.5 cm) stone chisel
- 2 tea light candles
- Bowl, 2 1/2 x 12 inches (6.4 x 30.5 cm)
- Collar, with 3 notches for pump cord and water circulation
- Hacksaw
- Miter box, optional
- Submersible pump
- Clear plastic tubing, to fit pump spout
- Small stones
- Plants or flowers, real or silk

1. Draw a 3 1/2-inch (8.9 cm) circle on the top side of the slate at its center point. At any attractive location on the slate away from its edge, draw two 1 1/2-inch (3.8 cm) circles for the tea light candles, and one small hole for the plant or flower.

2. Wearing the safety goggles, dust mask, and work gloves, use the diamond wheel on the drill or the small motorized rotary tool to grind out the 3 1/2-inch (8.9 cm) circle into a bowl shape. If available, use the 4-inch (10.2 cm) grinder with the masonry grinding wheel first to remove as much slate as possible. Apply more pressure in the center of the bowl and lighten up toward the edges. Grind the slate in a circular motion to keep all sides even until reaching the desired depth. Vary the diameter of the bowl as much as you like, but never penetrate all the way through the slate. Use the masonry bit to drill a hole in the center of the bowl you just created.

3. Wearing the safety goggles, dust mask, and work gloves, use the carbide grit hole saw to drill partial holes, or *seats*, for the tea lights. Don't drill all the

way through the slate. Chisel inside each ring, leaving a seat for the candle. Use the small diamond grinding wheel if needed to widen the hole. The tea light candles should sit flush with the top of the slate. Use the masonry bit to drill the hole for the plant or flower.

4 The slate needs to tilt slightly forward in the bowl for proper water flow. There are two ways to position the slate on the collar in the bowl:

The first method is to use the hacksaw to cut the collar the same height as the bowl. Adjust the pump's water flow regulator to its lowest setting. Slide the plastic tubing over the pump spout and form a tight seal. Place the pump and the collar in the bowl. Fill the bowl with enough water to cover the pump's intake valve. Feed the plastic tubing through the center hole in the slate. Slide the slate down the tubing until it's supported by the bowl edges and the collar. Slightly lift the back of the slate. Shim the tilted slate by wedging slate chips between the collar and underside of the slate. Cut the plastic tubing flush with the top of the hole, and conceal it with an arrangement of small stones. Turn on the pump to test the fountain's water flow and pressure. Adjust the shims as needed to produce more or less of an angle for the slate. Add stones to the top of the slate and a silk plant or fresh flower.

For the second option, follow the process described above, except cut the collar to the appropriate angle. This eliminates the need for shims. Without the collar in the bowl, feed the tubing through the center hole in the slate. Slide the slate down until it rests on the bowl edges. At the front of the bowl, measure the height from the base to the underside of the slate. Slightly tilt the slate, and measure the height between the base of the bowl and the underside of the lifted edge. Measure and mark these two points on opposite sides of the collar. Use a miter box with the hacksaw to precisely cut the angle in the collar.

Parlor Fountain

Blue and white is a classic color combination for ceramics. Although the designer found the decorative elements in a contemporary home accessory store, you may discover interesting items scavenging weekend flea markets and antique shops. Ornamental orbs in ceramic, glass, or metal are a great catch for fountain enthusiasts.

Submersible pump

Clear plastic tubing, to fit
pump spout

Ceramic bowl, 6 x 8 inches
(15.2 x 20.3 cm)

Collar, with 3 notches for cord and
water circulation

4 or 5 ceramic spheres, 3 inches
(7.6 cm) in diameter

1 Adjust the pump's water flow regulator to its lowest setting. Place the clear plastic tubing over the pump spout and form a tight seal. Position the pump on the base of the bowl, with the spout at its center. Set the collar over the pump, running its electrical cord under a notch.

2 Make a balanced and secure arrangement of the decorative spheres both inside the bowl and extending over its rim. Center the spheres around the plastic tubing. Run the pump cord over the back of the bowl, hiding it between spheres.

3 Cut the plastic tubing so it's out of view, approximately 1 $^1\!/_2$ inches (3.8 cm) below the top layer of spheres. Add enough water to the bowl to cover the pump's intake valve. Turn the pump on and observe the water flow, adjusting the pump pressure as needed.

air plants

A gardener who works with *aerophytes* or *epiphytes* won't get dirty. Although air plants, as they're commonly known, need light and water like other flora, they don't grow in soil! This fact, combined with the minimal care they need, makes air plants ideal accents for tabletop fountains.

Air plant roots don't take in food, but just act as anchors. Air plants may attach themselves to other plants or trees, but don't feed off them like parasites. Instead, air plants have specialized leaves that absorb moisture and nutrients from air and rainwater. Tiny scales on the leaf, called *trichomes*, assist the plant's feeding by holding greater amounts of water against the leaf surface for a longer period of time. Trichomes also reflect the intense sunlight that's common in the growing environment of these plants. Finally, trichomes give many of the air plants their characteristic gray color.

Many air plants are tropical, and favor shady but warm conditions. You can determine the growing requirements of these plants by their appearance. Plants with a dense covering of scales on their leaves prefer bright light and little water. A plant with glossy leaves needs lower light and higher humidity.

Aerophytes are hardy plants. They can survive temperatures ranging from 35° to 120° F (3° to 88° C). They can tolerate long periods without water, but at the same time, they run little risk of overwatering. Once a week, simply soak your air plants in water. Air plants also appreciate a periodic misting of their foliage.

Because they don't take root, air plants are a versatile addition to a fountain. You can move them around at will: perch one on a rock, drape it over an element, or hang it from a delicately wrought hook. Air plants even bloom, and the tips of their leaves turn pink, orange, and red prior to this delightful display.

did you know?

Concolor

Please note that aerophytes should not be collected in the wild. Purchase plants, seeds, and cuttings from well-stocked nurseries.

popular air plants

Look for some of these air plants, which mainly bloom from fall to spring:

Ionantha has tall, thin leaves. Its center turns a fiery red-pink before giving small purple blooms. A dwarf plant, in nature Ionantha seldom grows more than 2 inches (5 cm) in diameter.

Caput-Medusa's swirling arms flow up from a bulbous base. Its tall coral-red spikes produce purple flowers. It can reach a height of more than 10 inches (25.4 cm).

Concolor has stiff, wide leaves like those atop a pineapple. Pink flowers bloom from its red spikes. It grows over 8 inches (20.3 cm) tall.

Aeranthos is a bushy plant with stiff, sturdy leaves. It blooms purple after turning pink, and grows to about 4 inches (10.2 cm).

Tenuifolia has deep green leaves that resemble the fronds of a palm tree. Its spectacular magenta and purple blossoms measure about 2 inches (5 cm) long. This plant reaches 6 inches (15.2 cm).

Usneoides, also known as Spanish moss, has curly leaves that range from silver to soft green to tan. It gives yellowish-green or blue flowers, and can reach lengths of more than 25 feet (7.7 m).

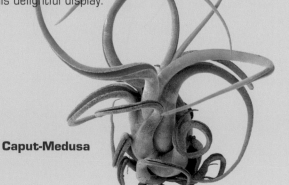

Caput-Medusa

Designer: Tony Estrada

Harmony Fountain

This fountain has a strong and sophisticated presence. Water streams down, pipe by pipe, finally dropping lightly onto the polished stones surrounding the chiseled slate surface. The fine lines of tall ornamental grasses add a quiet elegance.

Bowl, 4 x 10 inches (10.2 x 25.4 cm)

Slate tile, larger than top of bowl

Safety goggles

Work gloves

Stone chisel

Hammer

Collar, with 3 notches for pump cord
and water circulation

Dust mask

Masonry drill bit, same diameter as plastic tubing

Variable speed drill

Pipe cutter or metal hacksaw

Miter box, optional

Copper pipe, $3/4$ x 8 inches (1.9 x 20.3 cm)

Copper pipe, 1 x 8 inches (2.5 x 20.3 cm)

Copper pipe, 1 x 7 inches (2.5 x 17.8 cm)

Copper pipe, 2 x 9 inches (5 x 22.9 cm)

Poly-foam, 6 x 6 x $3/8$ inches (15.2 x 15.2 x 1 cm)

Clear plastic tubing, to fit pump spout

Thin copper sheeting, 26 gauge or less, 6 x 6
inches (15.2 x 15.2 cm), optional

Metal shears, optional

Metal drill bit, optional

Small motorized rotary tool, optional for patina

Metal grinding bits, optional for patina

Patina solution or propane torch, optional

Submersible pump

Zip tie, 12 inches (30.5 cm) long

Modeling clay

China marker

Sandpaper

Waterproof epoxy

Acrylic paint, copper or brown

Small paintbrush

Spray lacquer varnish

Polished river stones

Plants or flowers, real or silk

1 Place the bowl upside down on top of the slate, and trace the outline of the bowl. Put the slate on a concrete surface. Wearing the safety goggles and work gloves, chisel the slate to fit inside the top of the bowl. Begin at one edge of the slate and chisel in $1/2$-inch (1.3 cm) increments to avoid splitting the slate. Test fit the chiseled slate by placing the collar in the center of the bowl and resting the slate on top. If needed, trim the collar with a hacksaw until the slate sits flush with the top of the bowl. Wearing the safety goggles, dust mask, and work gloves, use the masonry bit to drill a hole at the center point of the slate.

2 With the pipe cutter or hacksaw, cut the $3/4$ x 8-inch (1.9 x 20.3 cm) copper pipe at a 40° angle to make a 3-inch (7.6 cm) and a 5-inch (12.7 cm) length. Use the pipe cutter or hacksaw to cut the same angle from one end of the remaining pipes.

preparing the pipes

3 Place the flat end of the 9-inch (22.9 cm) copper pipe near a corner on the poly-foam. Firmly press the pipe down while slightly wiggling it to incise the foam. Cut out the embossed shape. Repeat this process for all other pipes. Make an incision at the center of the 2-inch (5 cm) circle of foam for the plastic tubing. A tight fit is desirable.

4 If you wish, use the copper sheeting to disguise the foam in the tops of the pipes. Stand the flat end of one pipe on top of the copper sheeting. Trace around the pipe with a pencil. Repeat this process for each piece of pipe. Cut out the traced circles with the metal shears. Wearing the safety goggles, dust mask, and work gloves, use the metal bit to drill a hole in the center of the 2-inch (5 cm) copper circle for the plastic tubing. If available, use a small motorized rotary tool with a metal grinding bit to make the hole.

5 If you want to give the copper pipes a patina finish, apply a commercial patina solution following the manufacturer's directions, or flame torch the copper. Remove the foam and the copper center pieces from the pipes before flame torching. When the copper pipes reach the desired color, scuff their surface with the metal grinder to bring back shiny highlights.

postioning the pipes

6 Adjust the pump's water flow regulator to its lowest setting. Attach the plastic tubing to the pump spout and form a tight seal. Place the pump and the collar in the center of the bowl. Feed the plastic tubing through the center hole in the slate and rest the slate on the collar. Place the 9-inch (22.9 cm) copper pipe over the plastic tube. Measure and mark the plastic tubing 1 inch (2.5 cm) below the front (lowest point) of the top of the copper pipe. Remove the copper pipe and cut the plastic tubing at the marked line. Slide the poly-foam and copper sheeting circle (if using) over the plastic tube, and push them down 1 inch. Feed the 9-inch copper pipe over the tubing, foam, and copper. Wedge the cut foam, then the copper sheeting circles (if using) inside the tops of the remaining pipes. Slide the foam and copper sheeting circles down 1 to 2 inches (2.5 to 5 cm) inside the pipes.

7 Turn the 9-inch (22.9 cm) copper pipe to face the front of the slate. Position the 7-inch (17.8 cm) pipe in front of the 9-inch pipe. Turn the 7-inch pipe slightly inward. Place the 5½-inch (14 cm) pipe to the side of the 7-inch pipe, and turn it slightly inward. Put the 3-inch (7.6 cm) pipe in front of the 5½-inch pipe and turn it slightly inward. The 8-inch (20.3 cm) pipe is the plant holder. It goes behind the 5½-inch pipe. It's turned slightly outward. Place it with the group of pipes after the next step is complete.

8 Wrap the zip tie around the bottom of the copper pipe arrangement to hold it together. Stick modeling clay in the gap where the 9-, 7-, and 5½-inch (22.9, 17.8, and 14 cm) pipes meet. Put more clay where the 7-, 5½-, and 3-inch (17.8, 14, and 7.6 cm) pipes meet. These two gaps will later be filled with epoxy. The modeling clay helps with the initial testing of the water flow.

9 Fill the bowl with enough water to cover the pump's intake valve, and plug in the pump cord. The goal is to find the correct angles of the pipes to have the water fill each one. The water flowing from the top of the 9-inch (22.9 cm) pipe should fall evenly into the 7- and 5½-inch (17.8 and 14 cm) pipes. The pump pressure, height of the plastic tubing, and the copper tube positioning all factor into achieving the ideal water flow. Trial and error is the best way to reach the proper conditions, and here are a few suggestions: It's helpful if the plastic tubing is slightly curved. If so, turn the top of the tubing toward the 5½-inch pipe. Rotate the pipes to adjust their position without removing the zip tie. Reposition the modeling clay if needed. For additional splash control, push the foam and the copper sheeting circles further down from the tops of the pipes.

securing the pipes

10 Once you've found the best arrangement, use a china marker to make vertical lines indicating where the pipes meet. For example, draw a line on the front of the 9-inch (22.9 cm) pipe that extends straight down into the interior of the 7-inch (17.8 cm) pipe. These lines will be realigned later. Make as many marks as needed to assist you in correctly fitting the tubes back together.

11 Remove the zip tie and modeling clay. Slide the 9-inch (22.9 cm) pipe off the plastic tubing. Use the sandpaper to scuff the areas on the pipes that will be joined with epoxy. Mix only enough epoxy to glue one tube at a time. Start with the 7-inch (17.8 cm) pipe. Lay a straight $1/8$ x 7-inch (.3 x 17.8 cm) line of epoxy onto the pipe where it joins the 9-inch pipe. Make sure all marks are aligned and the pipe bottoms are even. Press the two pieces together tightly to avoid a gap. It helps to slightly slide the pipes back and forth while firmly pressing them together. Wipe away any excess epoxy, then let it dry. Repeat this bonding process for the $5 1/2$-inch (14 cm) to the 7-inch pipe, then to the 9-inch pipe. Use the epoxy to create a small downward slope in the corner gap where the water flows into the $5 1/2$-inch pipe from the 9-inch (22.9 cm) pipe. Repeat the bonding process for the 3-inch (7.6 cm) pipe without creating a slope in the corner gap. Epoxy the 8-inch (20.3 cm) copper pipe flower holder in position. Once all the epoxy is completely dry, paint it with the copper or brown acrylic to match the pipe. Let the paint dry. Spray the copper pipes with the lacquer varnish to preserve the patina finish. Let the varnish dry.

12 Place the copper pipe fountain element over the plastic tubing, foam, and copper sheeting circles. Refill the bowl with water if needed, and plug in the pump cord. Arrange polished river stones on top of the slate, around the base of the pipes. Add a plant or flower to the holder.

59

Mosaic Fountain

Creating a mosaic vessel is fun. Turning that vessel into a tabletop fountain doubles your pleasure. Whether you're an experienced mosaic artist or a complete beginner, this project is simple to create. Choose to work with a myriad of rainbow colors or a single palette—whatever strikes your fancy!

What You Need

- Safety goggles
- Tile nippers
- 6 or 8 ceramic plates
- Terra-cotta planter bowl
- Premixed ceramic tile adhesive
- Flat poly-foam trays
- Plastic knife or palette knife
- 1/2 cup (168 g) sanded grout
- Plastic container for mixing grout
- Disposable latex gloves
- Polyethylene foam sheeting, cut into 4-inch (10.2 cm) pieces
- Plastic tub or bucket for water
- Waterproofing solution for ceramics
- Submersible pump
- Clear plastic tubing, to fit pump spout
- Fountain container
- Collar, with 3 notches for pump cord and water circulation
- Tumbled ceramic shards

1 Wearing the safety goggles, use the tile nippers to break the ceramic plates in half. Continue to break the plates into smaller and smaller pieces. Your goal is to create ceramic pieces measuring close to 1/2 inch (1.3 cm). Reserve pieces from the plate rims in a separate pile. Separate them by color if you wish.

2 Trim the rim of the terra-cotta bowl with the 1/2-inch (1.3 cm) pieces of ceramic. Position the tiles 1/8 inch (3 mm) apart. Use the tile nippers to trim each piece to fit as needed. Spread the back of each piece with the ceramic tile adhesive. Adhere tiles first along the rim and the foot of the bowl. This gives your fountain a nice, finished edge. Cover the rest of the bowl's outer surface with pieces of ceramic, trimming pieces with the tile nippers to fit as needed. Let the bowl dry overnight.

61

then use clean pieces of polyethylene foam to wipe the surface clean, removing all excess grout on or between the ceramic pieces. Let the grouted mosaic set for 30 minutes, then use a damp cloth or sponge to remove all traces of excess grout. Let the bowl dry overnight.

4 After the grout has cured, coat the interior of the bowl with the waterproofing solution for ceramics, following the manufacturer's instructions. Let the sealer dry.

5 Slide the plastic tubing over the pump spout and form a tight seal. Adjust the pump's water flow regulator to its lowest setting. Place the pump with the tubing and the collar into the fountain container. Feed the plastic tubing through the hole in the mosaic bowl, and slide the bowl to rest on top of the collar. Use tumbled ceramic shards as fountain filler. Pour enough water into the fountain container to cover the pump's intake valve. Turn the pump on and observe the water flow. Alter the arrangement of the loose tumbled shards for visual and acoustic effect. Adjust the pump pressure as needed.

3 Mix the grout according to the manufacturer's instructions; it should be about the consistency of cake frosting or mashed potatoes. Wearing the gloves, use a piece of the polyethylene foam to spread the grout over the tile-covered surface of the bowl. Press the grout into the small spaces between the ceramic pieces until the bowl is well covered. Allow the grout to set for 15 minutes,

Designer: Marthe Le Van

Moss Grotto Fountain

The primeval look of this moss-embellished fountain brings to mind the
cool, damp, and enchanting interior of a stalagmite-rich cave. The moss,
half real and half artificial, fills three layers of stacked metal candleholders.
Replace the moss with a permanent filler for a low maintenance fountain.

3 metal pedestal candleholders,
4 x 7 inches (10.2 x 17.8 cm),
3 x 6 inches (7.6 x 15.2 cm),
2 1/2 x 4 inches (6.4 x 10.2 cm)

Vise grip

Safety goggles

Sturdy work gloves

Dust mask

Variable speed drill

Metal drill bit, same diameter as
plastic tubing

Submersible pump

Clear plastic tubing, to fit pump spout

Bowl, 3 1/2 x 10 inches
(8.9 x 25.4 cm)

Collar, non-weight-bearing,
with 3 notches for pump cord and
water circulation

Moss, real or artificial

1 Measure and mark the center point on the top surface of all three candleholders. Place one candleholder securely in the vise grip, and put on the safety goggles, dust mask, and sturdy work gloves. Using the metal bit, begin to drill on the lowest setting. Apply more pressure and drill speed as required to penetrate the surface of, and eventually make a hole through, the candleholder. To prevent the bit from slipping, you may want to start by drilling a pilot hole with a smaller diameter bit. Once the correct size hole is drilled, remove the candleholder from the vise grip. Repeat this process for the other two candleholders. Carefully clean all metal shavings off the candleholders, your work area, and gloves.

2 Adjust the pump's water flow regulator to its lowest setting. Place the clear plastic tubing over the pump spout and form a tight seal. Position the pump on the base of the bowl, with the spout at the center. Conceal and protect the pump with the collar. The collar need not be weight-bearing as no fountain element rests directly on the pump.

3 Feed the tubing through the hole in the large candleholder and slide it down so all its legs sit on the interior edges of the bowl. Repeat this process with the medium, then the small candleholder. Rotate the candleholders to face the desired direction, making sure they're level and sturdy.

4 Cut the end of the plastic tubing approximately $\frac{1}{2}$ inch (1.3 cm) above the top surface of the small candleholder. Add enough water to the bowl to cover the pump's intake valve. Arrange the moss on all three levels of the fountain, disguising the tubing as needed. Turn the pump on and observe the water flow. Adjust the moss and the pump's pressure for visual and acoustic appeal. Pulling small strands of moss over the rims of the candleholders will cause the water to flow in streams down the fountain's perimeter.

Designer: Marthe Le Van

Frosted Glass Fountain

The graceful beauty of clean lines, sheer color, and a spiral water
flow sets this fountain apart. It's lit from within by an underwater
bulb to illuminate every detail. It's simple to change the look of
this fountain by choosing an alternate light fixture or bowl.

Submersible pump

Clear plastic tubing, to fit pump spout and light fixture hole

Glass bowl with squared sloping edges, 3 x 12 inches (7.6 x 30.5 cm)

Collar, white or light opaque color, with 3 notches for pump cord and water circulation, non–weight–bearing

Glass light fixture cover, molded and etched, 4 x 8 inches (10.2 x 20.3 cm), or smaller than glass bowl

Tumbled glass or beach glass

Glass half marble

1 Adjust the pump's water flow regulator to its lowest setting. Place the clear plastic tubing over the pump spout and form a tight seal. Position the pump on the base of the bowl, with the spout at the center. Conceal and protect the pump with the white or light colored collar. The collar need not be weight-bearing as long as no fountain element rests directly on the pump.

2 Feed the tubing through the hole in the light fixture cover. Slide the light fixture down the tube to rest on the interior sides of the glass bowl. This fountain's molded-glass light fixture has a three-dimensional spiral pattern with a scalloped edge. The pump's electrical cord easily passes under this edge. The scallop also permits the falling water to circulate back into the bowl.

3 Cut the plastic tubing flush with the top of the hole in the light fixture cover. Telescope the tubing if needed to produce a tight fit with the light fixture's hole.

4 Pour water slowly through the seam between the glass bowl and light fixture. Add enough water to the bowl to cover the pump's intake valve. Cover the area where the glass bowl and light fixture meet with tumbled glass or beach glass. Turn the pump on and observe the water flow. Place the glass half marble on top of the light fixture's hole to soften the jet and evenly distribute the water around the spiraling, textured glass. Adjust the pump pressure as needed.

Designer: Paris Mannion

Seashore Memory Fountain

Enjoy the beach anytime! Adorned with treasures from the sea, this fountain stirs up memories of rustling sea grasses, pristine dunes, and refreshing waves. It's a great display for a shell collection, highlighting the magnificent shapes, colors, and textures found in nature.

What You Need

Round bowl, 3 x 9 inches (7.6 x 22.9 cm)

Slate tile, 12 x 12 x 1/2 inches (30.5 x 30.5 x 1.3 cm)

Cinder block

Work gloves

Hammer

Variable speed drill

Masonry drill bit, same diameter as plastic tubing

Large spiral shell, such as one from the murex or tulip family

Small motorized rotary tool

Cone-shaped ceramic tile bit for small motorized rotary tool

Dust mask

Safety goggles

Submersible pump

Clear plastic tubing, to fit pump spout

Waterproof epoxy or silicone sealant

Decorative stones and shells

Driftwood, optional

Air plant, optional

1 Lay one-third of the slate tile across the top of the round bowl. Draw a half circle that hangs 1/2 inch (1.3 cm) over the rim of the bowl.

2 Wearing the work gloves, hold the slate firmly on the cinder block. Position one corner of the slate so the area to be removed hangs over the cinder block 3/4 inch (1.9 cm) or less. Tap the overhanging portion with the hammer. Turn the slate to chip off another area, following the marked line. Continue chipping until the slate is a half circle or less, and fits over the back third of the bowl.

3 Determine a location for the shell on top of the slate—left, right, or center. Place the shell upside down so its lip extends past the edge of the slate and over the bowl. Mark the underside of the shell to indicate where to drill a hole for the plastic tubing. The hole must be far enough under the shell so water flows out of its lip, not over its side edge. Water flowing over the shell's side edge will travel sideways across the slate and land outside of the bowl.

4 Wearing the safety goggles, dust mask, and work gloves, use the cone-shaped ceramic bit with the small motorized rotary tool to begin drilling the marked shell. The bit will eventually catch and start to penetrate the shell. Dip the shell in water to keep it cool and reduce bad-smelling powder. Keep widening the hole until it's large enough to accept the clear plastic tubing.

5 Reposition the shell on the slate. Mark the slate to indicate where to drill a hole for the plastic tubing. Wearing the safety goggles, dust mask, and work gloves, use the masonry bit to drill a hole through the slate.

6 Adjust the pump's water flow regulator to its lowest setting. Place the clear plastic tubing over the pump spout and form a tight seal. Position the pump in the back of the bowl. Slide the slate hole over the plastic tubing, then run the pump cord between the slate and the rim of the bowl. Twist the tubing through the hole in the shell. The tubing should rise only $1/2$ inch (1.3 cm) above the shell. Remove the shell to trim the tubing if needed.

7 Hold the tubing in place and twist the shell off the tubing. Coat the inner and outer edges of the shell hole with the waterproof epoxy or silicone sealant. Add glue to the outside of the plastic tubing. Twist the shell back into place and let the glue dry.

8 Add enough water to the bowl to cover the pump's intake valve. Arrange various rocks or shells on the bottom of the bowl as decorative accents, and to hide the pump. Plug in the pump cord. The water will travel up the tubing, fill the shell, overflow its lip, and fall back into the bowl. Reseal the juncture of the tubing and the shell if water leaks. Adjust the pump pressure as needed.

9 Decorate the top of the slate, and around the shell as desired. This is a great place to display your personal collection from the beach. Other accents such as driftwood, air plants, and polished stones also add charm. To alter the sound of the fountain, position a rock underneath the water flowing from the shell.

Designer: Susan Kieffer

Avalon Ice Fountain

The inventive design of this fountain is inspiring, unifying water in its
three states—liquid, solid, and gas. Even though the fountain is exotic,
it's also functional and flexible. An ice fountain as the centerpiece for
your next party is sure to be a hit. The water can be tinted to match
your decorations or filled with flower petals.

Large tin can, 7 inches (17.8 cm) tall

Blue food coloring, optional

Clear plastic tubing, 9 inches (22.9 cm) long, to fit pump spout

Copper tubing, 15 inches (38.1 cm) long, to fit inside clear plastic tube

Freezer

5 shallow decorative molds, 3 to 4 inches (7.6 to 10.2 cm) in diameter

Submersible pump

Rigid plastic collar, 4 inches (10.2 cm) in diameter, with 3 notches for pump cord and water circulation

Clear glass bowl, at least 11 inches (27.9 cm) in diameter

Clear plastic tubing, 2 inches (5 cm) long

Plastic plant underliner, 8 inches (20.3 cm) in diameter

Copper tube, 3 inches (7.6 cm) long, to fit inside clear plastic tube

Ice pick

Clear or pale blue marbles, or tumbled glass shards

Dry ice

Leafy plant foliage

1 Fill the tin can with $4\frac{1}{2}$ to 5 inches (11.4 to 12.7 cm) of water. Tint the water with the blue food coloring, if desired. To prevent the 9-inch (22.9 cm) plastic tubing from collapsing when the water is frozen, insert the 15-inch (38.1 cm) copper tube into the plastic tubing.

2 Position the water-filled can near the center of a freezer shelf. Tilt the can so the water level on one side rises up to the lip of the can. Support the can with items in the freezer so it won't tip over. Place the plastic tubing into the can parallel to and approximately 1 inch (2.5 cm) away from the can's high-water side. To keep the tubing in position while the water freezes, use a twist tie to secure the tubing to a freezer shelf above the can, or insert the tubing between the shelf grid above the can. Fill the little molds with water and place them in the freezer. Freeze all fountain elements overnight, or until solid.

3 Adjust the pump's water flow regulator to its lowest setting. Position the collar over the pump, and put them in the clear glass bowl. Slide the 2-inch (5 cm) piece of plastic tubing over the pump spout, and form a tight seal. Cut an off-center hole in the plastic plant underliner, and place it over the 2-inch (5 cm) piece of plastic tubing. Insert the 3-inch (7.6 cm) copper tube into the 2-inch (5 cm) plastic tube.

4 Remove the can from the freezer and run warm water over the outside to loosen the ice from the mold. Using the ice pick, chip approximately 1 inch (2.5 cm) of ice away from the bottom of the mold to expose the plastic tubing. Pick away any ice blocking the bottom of the tubing if needed. Pull the thin copper tube out of the plastic tube.

5 Place the large ice block onto the plastic plant underliner, inserting the pump's copper tube into the ice block's plastic tube. Trim the tubing that protrudes from the top of the ice block to approximately 3/4 inch (1.9 cm). Unmold the smaller ice decorations. Use the ice pick to shave a small hole in the center of one of the molded shapes. Place this ice decoration over the tubing at the top of the fountain head. Slightly wet the other molded ice forms. Position them around the sides of the fountain head, approximately 2 inches (5 cm) down from the top, and hold each one until it sticks. Place the marbles or tumbled glass shards in the plastic plant underliner and the bowl. Fill the bowl with enough water to cover the pump's intake filter. Arrange the greenery in the bowl and turn on the pump. Scatter approximately 1 cup (24 mL) of the dry ice on the water in the bowl.

Designer: Tony Estrada

Bamboo Fountain

Bamboo is a symbolic and versatile plant often found in fountain designs. Here, bamboo is used with great imagination to form a double-spout for water flow. For a special effect, two rock basins—originally votive candle-holders—collect and pool the streaming water.

What You Need

- **Oblong bowl, 3 x 15 x 13 inches (7.6 x 38.1 x 33 cm)**
- **Slate tile, larger than bowl**
- **Safety goggles**
- **Work gloves**
- **Stone chisel**
- **Hammer**
- **Collar, with 3 notches for pump cord and water circulation**
- **Wide piece of dried bamboo, 10 inches (25.4 cm) long**
- **Narrow piece of dried bamboo, 11 inches (27.9 cm) long**
- **Variable speed drill**
- **Wood drill bit, same diameter as plastic tubing**
- **Handsaw**
- **Waterproof epoxy or silicone**
- **Raffia**
- **Dust mask**
- **Masonry drill bit, large diameter**
- **Small diamond grinding wheel**
- **Small motorized rotary tool, optional**
- **Poly-foam, small piece, 3/8 inch (9.5 mm) thick**
- **Submersible pump**
- **Clear plastic tubing, to fit pump spout**
- **2 stone tea light candleholders, or ceramic cups**
- **River stones**
- **Plant or flowers, real or silk**

1 Place the oblong bowl upside down on top of the slate and trace the outline of the bowl. Put the slate on a concrete surface. Wearing the safety goggles and work gloves, chisel the slate to fit inside the top of the bowl. To avoid splitting the slate, begin at one edge and work toward the marked line in ½-inch (1.3 cm) increments. Test fit the chiseled slate by placing the collar in the center of the bowl and resting the slate on top. Reposition or trim the collar with a hacksaw so the slate sits flush with the top of the bowl.

2 Wearing the safety goggles and work gloves, use the wood bit to drill out growth rings inside the bamboo. Measure, mark, then use the handsaw to cut the narrow bamboo into a 6-inch (15.2 cm) and a 5-inch (12.7 cm) length. (See the bamboo sidebar on page 29.)

3 Measure 2 ½ inches (6.4 cm) down from the top of the wider, 10-inch (25.4 cm) piece of bamboo, and mark this point with a pencil. Hold one edge of

5 Make a mark at the center bottom edge of the 6-inch (15.2 cm) cross-piece. Use the wood bit to drill a hole only through the bottom edge of the bamboo.

6 Slide the 6-inch (15.2 cm) cross-piece, drilled hole down, through the drilled hole in the wide bamboo. Center the cross-piece and rotate if needed so the shortest edge is at the top. Apply a small amount of the waterproof epoxy or silicone around the seams where the bamboo pieces connect. Let the glue dry. Wrap the juncture with the raffia in an "X" pattern, then tie off the ends of the raffia in back. Apply a dab of glue to the raffia knot to prevent unraveling.

the 6-inch (15.2 cm) piece of bamboo on the center of the pencil mark. Trace the outline of the narrow bamboo onto the wider bamboo. Use the wood bit to drill the marked hole all the way through the wide bamboo. The narrow cross-piece should fit through this hole as tightly as possible.

7 Hold the base of the wide bamboo on the center point of the chiseled slate, and trace its outline. Wearing the safety goggles, dust mask, and work gloves, use the large masonry bit to drill a hole in the slate at the center of the bamboo's outline. Use the diamond wheel on the drill, or the small motorized rotary tool, to widen the hole. The bamboo piece needs to fit tightly into the hole to stand upright on its own, so periodically check its fitting. If the hole becomes too big, epoxy the inside edges.

4 With the handsaw, cut a 45° angle from one end of the cross-piece. Turn over the bamboo and cut a 45° angle from the opposite end. The reversed angles result in one longer edge of bamboo which is the bottom of the cross-piece. Saw a 45° angle from the top of the 10-inch (25.4 cm) bamboo piece.

8 Use the handsaw to cut an angle on one side of the 5-inch (12.7 cm) piece of bamboo. Repeat Step 7 for the 5-inch piece of bamboo, but drill its hole on one rear corner of the chiseled slate.

10 Adjust the pump's water flow regulator to its low-est setting. Position the pump in the center of the bowl. Slide the plastic tubing over the pump spout and form a tight seal. Place the collar over the pump. Fill the bowl with enough water to cover the pump's intake valve, then feed the tubing through the slate's center hole. Measure and cut the tubing 5 inches (12.7 cm) higher than the top of the slate. Feed the plastic tubing through the cut poly-foam. Push the foam down the tubing 1 inch (2.5 cm). Slide the base of the wide bamboo over the poly-foam and the tubing, then into the center hole in the slate. Insert the 5-inch bamboo piece into the rear hole on the slate. Place a stone tea light holder on top of the slate under each side of the bam-boo cross-piece. Display river stones and plants or flowers as desired. Turn on the pump and increase the pressure if needed.

9 Place the bottom of the 10-inch (25.4 cm) bam-boo piece on top of the poly-foam and trace its out-line, or firmly press the bamboo into the foam so it makes an impression. Cut out the shape with scissors, then make a narrow incision in the cen-ter of the foam for the plastic tubing. The foam piece must be snug both around the tubing and inside the bamboo.

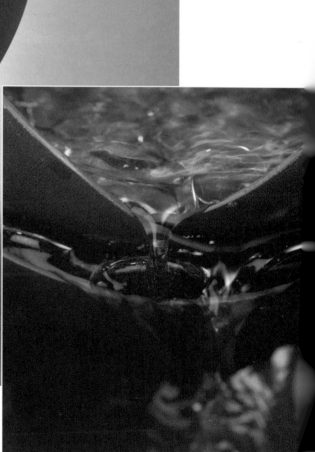

Designer: Marthe Le Van

Mod Tulip Fountain

This fun fountain converts mass-produced objects into contemporary art. Whoever thought that, turned at the right angles, four red salad bowls could resemble a tulip? Plastic is a great fountain material because it's waterproof and easy to drill.

4 plastic salad bowls, each approximately 2 ¹/₂ x 5 inches (6.4 x 12.7 cm), with gently scalloped edges

Safety goggles

Work gloves

Variable speed drill

Drill bit suitable for plastic, same diameter as plastic tubing

Plastic serving bowl, approximately 5 ¹/₂ x 9 inches (14 x 22.9 cm), with gently scalloped edges

Submersible pump

Clear plastic tubing, to fit pump spout

Clear glass half-marbles

1 Measure and mark the center point on the underside of one plastic salad bowl. This bowl will be positioned upside down in the center of the serving bowl, acting as the pump's fountain head.

2 Play with the three other salad bowls, arranging them at different angles, until you discover a pleasing design. Keep in mind that the plastic tubing must run through a point on all of the bowls. Mark this point on the bottom of each bowl. Mark the bowls as needed to remember the way they fit together.

3 Wearing the safety goggles and work gloves, position the fountain head bowl upside down on your work surface. Tightly grip the bowl as you drill a hole through the marked point. Plastic is a quick and easy material to drill, so proceed with caution. Too much pressure and speed applied too quickly can cause the bit to travel through the bowl and into your work surface. Repeat this step for the three remaining salad bowls.

4 Adjust the pump's water flow regulator to its lowest setting. Place the clear plastic tubing over the pump spout and form a tight seal. Position the pump on the base of the serving bowl, with the spout at the center.

5 Feed the plastic tubing through the hole in the fountain head bowl from the top. Slide the bowl over the pump until it rests on the base of the serving bowl. The pump cord needs to exit the bowl under one of its raised scalloped edges. String the rest of the plastic bowls onto the tubing according to the sequence you determined in Step 2. Rotate the bowls to re-create your original design.

6 Add enough water to the serving bowl to cover the pump's intake valve. Place clear glass half marbles in the top two bowls. Turn the pump on and observe the water flow. Adjust the half marbles and raise the pump pressure as needed.

Designer: Alan D. Otterson

Wind Chime Fountain

A coiled copper pipe wrapped with ivy is the central structure of this fountain, but it's the action of the fountain that's truly ingenious. Not only is the soft sound of water present, but also the casual melody of the chimes. The fountain's basin is a great place to feature extraordinary rocks and moss.

What You Need

- **Round bowl, 2 to 4 x 14 to 16 inches (5 to 10.2 x 35.6 to 40.6 cm)**
- **Polished river rocks, various sizes**
- **Clear lacquer, optional**
- **Coiled copper tubing, refrigerator-style, 1/2-Inch (1.3 cm) OD**
- **Coiled copper tubing, refrigerator-style, 3/8-inch (9.5 mm) OD**
- **Wind chimes with clapper, small**
- **Metal tubing cutter, optional**
- **Hacksaw**
- **Submersible pump**
- **Clear plastic tubing, 1/2-inch (1.3 cm) OD**
- **Clear plastic tubing, 5/8-inch (1.6 cm) OD**
- **Garland of real or artificial ivy**

1 Clean the bowl and the river rocks. Wipe any residue off the copper tubing. To keep the copper bright and shiny, apply a layer of clear lacquer following the manufacturer's directions.

2 Choose one special, large stone to put under the chime as a splash guard. Place the 1/2-inch (1.3 cm) OD copper tubing flat on the bottom of the bowl. Holding down the perimeter of the tubing with one hand, gently pull the center of the coil up in the air until it reaches the height required to hang the wind chime above the chosen rock. Hold the wind chime up to the top of the copper coil often as the tube is stretched. Mark the copper tube to indicate where to install the wind chime.

3 Cut off any excess tubing from the top of the stretched coil with the tubing cutter or hacksaw. Spread out the base of the coil until it fits the interior edge of the bowl.

4 At the mark made in Step 2, use the hacksaw to cut a slight notch or groove on top of the copper tube. Keep your cut shallow. A deep cut will wear and eventually break the wind chime cord.

5 Make a fountain spout from the $\frac{3}{8}$-inch (9.5 mm) copper tubing. Determine the spout length by measuring the height from the base of the bowl to the center of the wind chime clapper. Bend the copper tubing at an angle so its water flow will hit the clapper. Remove any excess tubing with the hacksaw or pipe cutter.

6 Slide the $\frac{5}{8}$-inch (1.6 cm) plastic tubing over the pump spout and make a tight connection. Cut the tubing at the point where it clears the pump spout by approximately $\frac{1}{2}$ inch (1.3 cm). Cut a short piece of the $\frac{1}{2}$-inch (1.3 cm) plastic tubing to fit inside the larger tubing, and install it over the pump spout. Insert the $\frac{3}{8}$-inch (9.5 mm) bent copper spout into the telescoped tubing.

7 Hang the wind chimes in the notch at the top of the copper tubing stand already in the bowl. Position the pump where the water from the spout will hit the chime's clapper. Add enough water to the bowl to cover the pump's intake valve. Turn on the pump and observe the water flow. Make adjustments as needed by changing the height of the wind chime stand, or altering the length and angle of the copper spout.

8 Cover the bottom of the bowl with small polished river rocks. Arrange the larger river rocks among the smaller ones for visual interest. Place the special rock (selected in Step 2) directly under the wind chime as a splash guard. The chime's clapper should hang just above the water level and the large rock. Disguise the pump with ivy. Line the perimeter of the bowl with a garland of ivy for visual appeal, and to serve as an excellent splash guard.

Slate Passage

A tranquil vista in miniature, this stacked slate fountain creates a gentle sound. Water cascades out an elevated spring and travels across peaks and valleys. Living culms of bamboo lend color to the environment and thrive in the fountain container.

What You Need

- Oval or rectangular bowl, 3 x 14 x 8 inches (7.6 x 35.6 x 20.3 cm)
- 2 slate tiles, each 12 x 12 x ½ inches (30.5 x 30.5 x 1.3 cm)
- Work gloves
- Cinder block
- Hammer
- Submersible pump
- Safety goggles
- Dust mask
- Variable speed drill
- Masonry drill bit, same diameter as plastic tubing
- Waterproof epoxy or silicone sealant
- Clear plastic tubing, to fit pump spout
- Large river stones
- Decorative pebbles
- Bamboo

1 Hold one slate tile over the bowl. Draw a line following the shape of the bowl but ½ inch (1.3 cm) smaller than the bowl's edges. This ½-inch (1.3 cm) gap lets water flow off the slate and into the bowl.

2 Wearing work gloves, firmly hold the slate on top of the cinder block. Starting at one corner, position the slate so the area to be removed hangs over the concrete block by about ½ inch (1.3 cm). Tap the overhanging portion of slate with the hammer.

Rotate the slate to chip off another area, following the line drawn. Continue chipping the slate until it's the right size for the bowl.

3 Break the second slate tile into large, irregular pieces by dropping it on the ground, or striking it at a 45° angle against the cinder block. Select one piece and shape it to fit one-third of the length across the support slate formed in Step 2.

4 Position the pump at one end of the bowl. Hold the support slate above the pump spout, and mark where to drill a hole for the pump spout and tubing. Wearing the safety goggles, dust mask, and work gloves, use the masonry bit to drill through the slate. Mark and drill the slate piece shaped in Step 3 so both holes align when stacked flush near one end of the bowl.

5 Break the leftover slate and sort the chips for colorful, flat pieces to be glued to the base slate. Select and clean about 20 pieces, wiping off grit with a sponge or cloth.

6 Apply the waterproof epoxy or silicone sealant around the drilled hole on the support slate. Set the smaller slate piece on top of the larger slate piece and align their holes. Add more glue around the back perimeter of the hole and construct an arrangement of slate chips. This new stack forms a barrier so water flows forward over the main support slate.

7 Glue more chips to the support slate. Form a slope by gradually decreasing the number of slate pieces as you work from the pump to the far end of the bowl. Let the glue dry.

8 Adjust the pump's water flow regulator to its lowest setting. Place the clear plastic tubing over the pump spout and form a tight seal. Position the pump at one end of the bowl, then position the large river stones at the opposite end of the bowl to support the weight of the slate. Slide the slate construction over the tubing. Rearrange the rocks so the slate is level, or dips slightly at the low end.

9 Add enough water to the bowl to cover the pump's intake valve, and plug in the cord. The water will bubble up, cover the slate surface, curl under its edge, and plop back into the bowl. Dress one corner of the bowl with bamboo cuttings, supporting them with decorative pebbles.

option

For added interest, create a slate island away from the fountain head. Stack and glue an attractive array of slate pieces onto the large foundation piece. This mound diverts the flow of water, providing visual and audible effects.

Love Eternal Fountain

This fountain has an aura of romance and fantasy. Segments of rose-colored stones convey nature's spectacular beauty. The water takes an attractive route down multiple tiers of polished stone in a gently soothing and peaceful manner.

What You Need

- PVC pipe, 1 1/2 inches (3.8 cm) in diameter
- Hacksaw or PVC cutter
- Round bowl, 3 1/2 x 12 inches (8.9 x 30.5 cm)
- Rainbow obsidian slab
- Rhodonite slab
- Hematite, 1/2 x 1 1/2 x 2 inches (1.3 x 3.8 x 5 cm)
- Waterproof epoxy
- 5 rigid plastic support rods, black, each 1/2 x 1/4 x 1/4 inch (1.3 x .6 x .6 cm)
- Rose quartz slab
- White agate slab
- Clear acrylic rod, such as a window blind rod
- 2 rigid clear plastic tubes, each 1 inch (2.5 cm) long, to hold the quartz and onyx points
- Rose quartz point (obelisk), 3 3/4 inches (9.5 cm) tall
- Black onyx point (obelisk), 3 3/4 inches (9.5 cm) tall
- Submersible pump
- Clear plastic tubing, telescoped if needed to fit the pump spout and agate hole
- Rose quartz, optional
- Incense burner, optional

1. Measure, mark, and cut the PVC pipe to sit flat on the base of the bowl. Place the rainbow obsidian and rhodonite slabs side by side on top of the pipe. Put the hematite on the front edge of the slabs at their seam. If needed, adjust the height of the pipe so the top of the hematite is the same height as the top of the bowl. Use the waterproof epoxy to glue the cut pipe to the base of the bowl, the two slabs to the top of the pipe, and the hematite at the slabs' seam. Let the epoxy dry.

2. Place one black plastic support rod on the back edge of each of the slabs glued in Step 1. Put a third rod behind the hematite. Position the rose quartz slab on top of these supports. Tilt the slab slightly so it touches the back edge of the hematite. This mild incline will propel the water forward. Adjust the height of the support rods if needed to accomplish this. Use waterproof epoxy to glue the support rods in place. Glue the top of the supports to the rose quartz slab. Prop up the back of the rose quartz slab while the glue dries.

adjust the lengths of the supports to produce a mild incline. Use waterproof epoxy to glue the black plastic supports and the clear acrylic rods in place. Let the glue dry.

4 Use waterproof epoxy to adhere the 1-inch (2.5 cm) tubes of rigid plastic under the rear edge of the rainbow obsidian and rhodonite slabs. Position one tube on either side of the rose quartz slab. Let the glue dry completely, then mount the rose quartz and black onyx points on top, securing them at the base with epoxy.

5 Adjust the pump's water flow regulator to its lowest setting. Slide the tubing over the pump's spout and form a tight seal. Place the pump on the rear base of the bowl. Insert the pump's tubing into the agate's hole. If needed, remove the pump and trim its tubing in small increments for a solid and well-balanced fit. Fill the bowl with enough water to cover the pump's intake valve, and turn on the fountain. Set the rose quartz on the agate over or near the fountain head to alter the flow of water, and increase the pump pressure as needed. Set an incense burner on top of the slabs if desired.

3 Place two black plastic support rods on the rear of the rose quartz slab, approximately $1/2$ inch (1.3 cm) from the edge and 2 inches (5 cm) apart. Set the white agate on top with one-third of its surface area hanging over the supports. Tilt the agate slab slightly, and measure the length from the base of the bowl to the underside of the agate slab at its outside edges. Cut two clear acrylic rods to this measurement, and position them under the agate slab with the plastic supports in place. If needed,

sound science

Water is essential for human life. But did you know that the sound of water can improve the quality of the life you live?

Acoustics, the science of sound, tells us that hearing is by no means the least of the five senses. Sound is a constant, and what you hear affects your mind and body's balance and equilibrium—whether you're conscious of it or not!

But where does water, and, specifically, your home fountain, fit in? Falling water appears to be the most soothing sound in nature. It has psychologically cooling and sleep-inducing effects. It soothes tension, promotes mental relaxation, and counteracts noise (any loud, discordant, or disagreeable sound). Tinkering with the design of your home fountain is an easy way to explore acoustics and take advantage of good vibrations!

Falling water owes its acoustic virtues to physics. Sound moves in waves. Irregular sound patterns are generally perceived as noise and have negative psychological impacts. A too-regular pattern also demands attention, making a nuisance of itself. The sound of water striking a surface offers regular but not too-regular patterns and varying frequencies. Voila! The result is a sound more soothing than complete silence—a serene sound your home fountain can reproduce.

Transform your fountain into a water orchestra by arranging any objects—stones, shells, dams, pools, canals, miniature figures, and structures—used in its design. The height of the water's fall, the way in which it spills, its flow, and the depth and size of obstructions shape the sound.

Before settling on a design, experiment. Construct a water obstacle course. Pour water from a wide decanter over a regular series of obstacles to create a constant sound. Notice how the water gurgles around certain shapes, drops to a gentle murmur on flat stretches, and rebounds to a babble as it cascades across a rough surface. Pour water from a narrow spout over an irregular arrangement that also varies in height to create a complex symphony.

Deep sounds cause a vibration in the bones reminiscent of a chant, and offer a similarly centering effect. High sounds travel further and suggest a singular, operatic quality. Once you have a feel for what tones each arrangement produces, set up your water pump and adjust the pressure to note how the increase or decrease in flow affects the sound. After some fine-tuning, you'll find the perfect arrangement of sounds to soothe and renew your spirit.

89

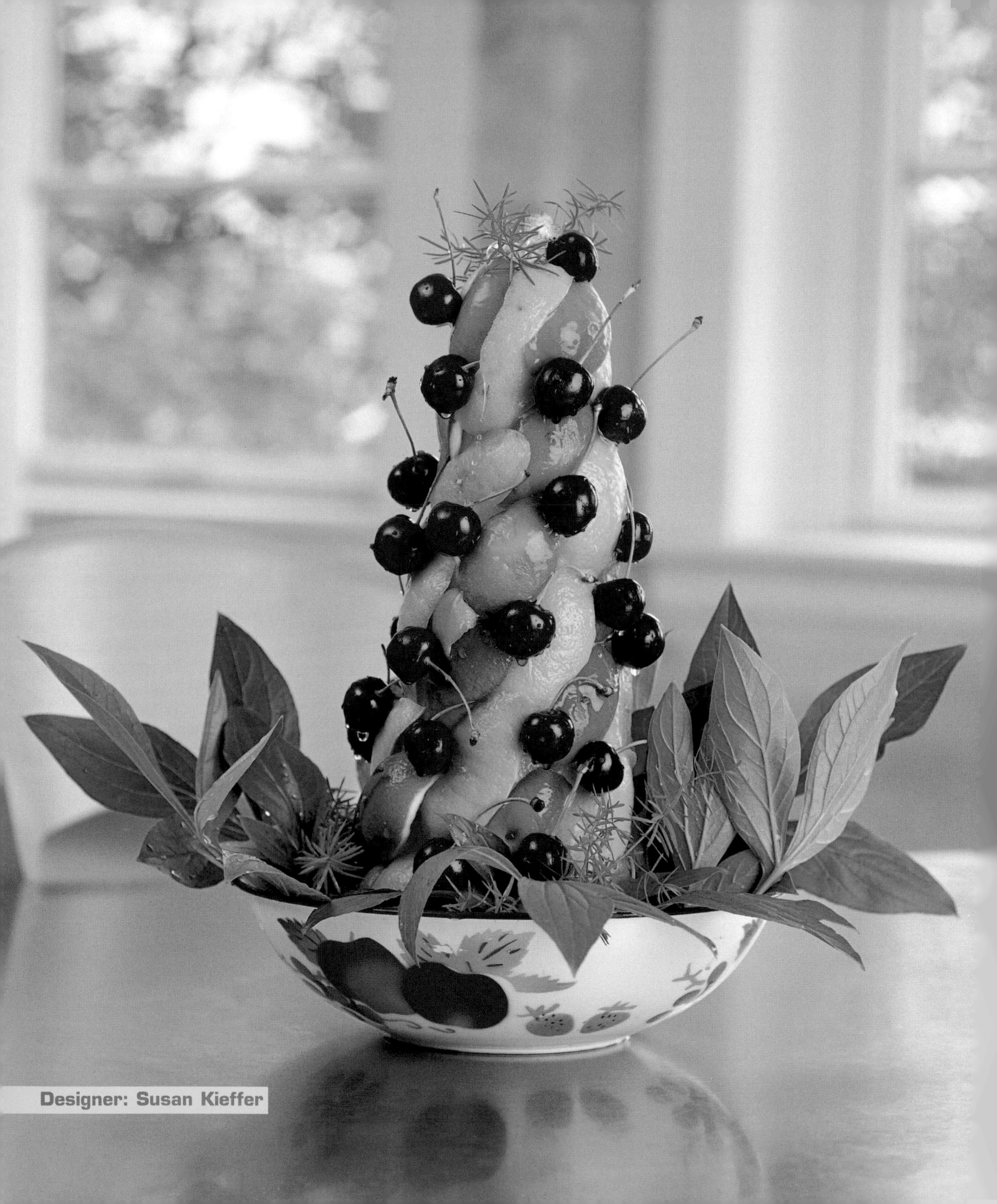

Designer: Susan Kieffer

Tropical Fruit Fountain

The perfect centerpiece for a summer soiree, this delectable fountain is sure to grab your guest's attention. The natural vibrant colors of real lemons, limes, and cherries are hard to beat, and their scented peels are an added bonus. The polyfoam cone base is easy to work with, so you'll have a new fountain in no time!

What You Need

Polyfoam cone, 5 inches (12.7 cm) in diameter, 15 inches (38.1 cm) high

Craft knife

Submersible pump

Clear plastic tubing, 15 inches (38.1 cm) long, to fit pump spout

Masking tape

Bowl, 4 to 5 inches (10.2 to 12.7 cm) deep

*5 lemons and 5 limes, approximate

Toothpicks

20 to 30 stemmed cherries

Sprigs of asparagus fern or parsley

Decorative foliage

* Smaller lemons and limes are easier to use for this project.

1 Measure, mark, and cut 2 inches (5 cm) off the pointed end of the polyfoam cone. Slice the cone in half lengthwise. Hollow out a channel for the plastic tubing to fit in the center and along the length of both cone sections. At the wide end of both cone halves, hollow out an area for the submersible pump.

2 Slide the plastic tubing over the pump spout and form a tight seal. Adjust the pump's water flow regulator to its lowest setting. Put the polyfoam cone halves back together around the pump and tubing. Position the pump cord between the seams of the cone. Holding the cone together, affix 4-inch (10.2 cm) sections of masking tape across the cut foam.

92

toothpicks. Position the ends of the lemon sections to touch or slightly overlap. Attach a row of lime sections next to the row of lemon sections. Repeat this process around the cone, alternating lemon and lime rows, until the cone is completely covered.

Cut off the protruding ends of the toothpicks flush with the fruit. Attach the cherries with toothpicks to fill in the open spaces on the cone. Snip the toothpicks flush with the fruit. Arrange a bit of the asparagus fern or parsley at the very top of the cone to camouflage any visible tubing. Arrange decorative leaves and more fern or parsley at the base of the cone. Plug in the pump, and observe the water flow.

Place the pump with the tubing and the cone into the bowl. Add enough water to the bowl to cover the pump's intake valve, and plug in the pump. Adjust the pump pressure as needed without causing the water to splash over the bowl edges.

Cut the lemons and limes into large wedge-like sections. Leave the pith and some of the flesh of the fruit on the sections. Starting at the top of the cone and working to the bottom in a spiraling manner, affix a row of lemon sections to the cone with

Jewel of the Pacific

This marine-inspired tableau features a whale's ascent over a coral reef, accented with blue agates and clear crystals. Water from the fountain splashes over the whale's back. Use varying sizes and colors of agates to alter the look and course of your fountain.

What You Need

2 PVC pipes, 1 and 1½ inches (2.5 and 3.8 cm) in diameter

Hacksaw, or PVC cutter

Coral

Glass whale, 24-karat gold tinted

Agate slabs, 2 solid, 1 with hole

Quartz cluster, large

Rainbow quartz, medium

Quartz point, rutilated

Clear acrylic rod, such as a window blind rod

Round bowl, 4 x 10 inches (10.2 x 25.4 cm)

Submersible pump

Waterproof epoxy

Clear plastic tubing, telescoped if needed to fit pump spout and agate hole

1 Measure, mark, and cut the 1½-inch (3.8 cm) PVC pipe to sit flat on the base of the bowl. Place the coral and the whale on top of the cut pipe to test the arrangement. Adjust the height of the pipe as needed to complement the depth of the bowl and the appearance of the fountain elements.

2 Measure, mark, and cut two pieces of the 1-inch (2.5 cm) PVC pipe to sit flat on the base of the bowl. Place (but don't glue) the two solid agates on top of the cut pipe, one on each side of the coral. Position one pipe with agate to the right of and slightly below the whale's head. Position the other pipe with agate toward the rear of the bowl, behind the whale's fluke.

3 Size two clear acrylic rods to support the top, holed agate. One rod should extend from each of the agates mounted in Step 2. Position the holed agate on top of the cut acrylic rods. Adjust the height of the rods to level the agate, and to enhance the composition of the fountain.

4 Determine the placement of the quartz pieces for both overall composition and anticipated water flow. In this fountain, the large quartz cluster is

mounted to both the rear, lowest agate and the coral. The medium rainbow quartz is mounted to the agate on the right, disguising a clear acrylic rod.

5 Join all fountain elements together at each intersecting seam with waterproof epoxy. Use at least two coats of glue on each joint, letting them dry between applications.

6 Slide the tubing over the pump spout and form a tight seal. Adjust the pump's water flow regulator to its lowest setting. Place the pump on the rear base of the bowl. Insert the pump's tubing into the top agate's hole. Remove the pump, and trim its tubing in small increments as needed for a solid fit and a balanced pump.

7 Place the rutilated quartz point on top of the highest quartz, over or near the fountain head. Leave this element unglued. Fill the bowl with enough water to cover the pump's intake valve and turn on the fountain. Increase the pump pressure if needed. Redirect the fountain's water flow by moving the loose quartz.

95

Designer: Tony Estrada

Treasured Artifact

You don't have to be an archeologist or spelunker to find this urn-shaped fountain absolutely fascinating. Viewed through a broken shard, it's lit from inside, and the water appears to seep through the rocks from the top. You'll enjoy putting a little extra effort into this fountain because it's as entertaining to make as it is to watch.

What You Need

- Ceramic pot, 14 x 8 x 8 inches, (35.6 x 20.3 x 20.3 cm), 5-inch (12.7 cm) diameter base and top rim
- Small motorized rotary tool
- Ceramic cutting bit for rotary tool
- Duct tape
- Submersible pump
- Candelabra light socket with cord
- Candelabra bulb, 25 watts or less
- Waterproof sealant for ceramics
- Inline power switch for pump cord
- Sandpaper
- Waterproof epoxy
- Silicone
- Copper pipe, same height as pot, 1/2 inch (1.3 cm) in diameter
- Pipe cutter or hacksaw
- Copper pipe T adapter, 1/2 inch (1.3 cm) in diameter
- Variable speed drill
- Metal drill bit, 1/8 inch (3 mm) in diameter
- Clear plastic tubing, to fit over both the copper pipe and the pump spout
- Various size stones
- Thin set mortar, rapid set preferable
- Acrylic add mix, optional
- Wooden mixing stick or old butter knife
- Small mixing bowl and water bowl
- Cotton-tipped swabs

preparing the pot

1 Draw a hole to cut out of the side of the pot. Begin the hole at least 3 inches (7.6 cm) from the bottom of the pot. Leave enough of the pot's top intact to hide the light bulb. Wearing the safety goggles and dust mask, use the ceramic cutting wheel in the small motorized rotary tool to cut the marked pot. Stop cutting once you reach the halfway point. Apply pieces of duct tape as needed to support the piece from falling through or breaking off as you work. Drill a small hole in the lower back of the pot for the pump's electrical cord. Drill a hole in the upper back of the pot for the light fixture. Clean all dust from the interior of the pot and apply the waterproof ceramic sealant. Double coat the bottom 3 inches (7.6 cm) of the pot. Let the sealant dry.

positioning and securing the cords

2 Adjust the submersible pump's water flow regulator to its lowest setting. Position the pump so its nozzle is in the center and against the back wall of the pot. Determine the location to cut the pump cord by keeping the pump in place and running the cord to the cord hole. Lengthen the cord, so the pump can still be pulled through the pot's front hole for cleaning. Add 2 inches (5 cm) to account for the inline switch in the back. Once the cord's measurement is determined, cut it and feed it through the hole. Use the sandpaper to roughen the cord at the point where it exits the hole. Install the inline switch onto the pump cord following the manufacturer's directions. Epoxy the pump cord hole on the interior and exterior of the pot. Once the

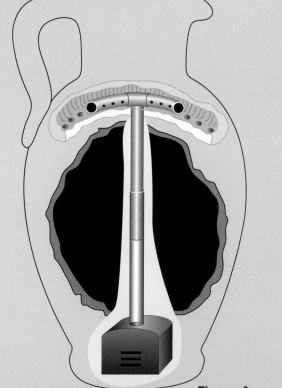

Figure 1

epoxy dries, apply silicone over the epoxy and cord. Install the power cord to the light socket if needed. Epoxy the light socket into its hole.

assembling and installing the copper pipe

3 Cut the 1/2-inch (1.3 cm) copper pipe to fit 3 inches (7.6 cm) above the pump spout and 2 to 3 inches (5 to 7.6 cm) below the light socket. Roughen the cut copper pipe and the copper T with the sandpaper, then epoxy them together. Wearing the safety goggles, dust mask, and work gloves, use the metal bit to drill two to three small 1/8-inch (3 mm) holes on the front surface of the copper T. With the copper T ends pointing to the sides of the pot, and the drilled holes facing front, bend the 1/2-inch copper pipe to match the curve of the back of the pot. Slide the 5-inch (12.7 cm) piece of plastic tubing over the bottom of the copper pipe and push it up 2 inches. This leaves 3 inches of flexible plastic tube at the bottom of the pipe. Slip the tube over the pump spout. While it's connected to the pump, center the copper pipe in the pot. Mark the location of the copper T at the top of the pot, and draw a line along both sides of the pipe. Extend a straight and even line from each side of the copper T's holes. Run these lines one-quarter of the distance around the pot on both sides. These lines indicate the placement of the epoxy trough through which the water channels once it exits the copper T (see figure 1).

4 Remove the pump from the plastic tube. Mix enough epoxy to secure the copper pipe and the copper T. Apply epoxy to the entire length of the copper tube where the markings were made. The plastic tube should not be able to slide.

creating an epoxy trough

5 Mix more epoxy for the water channel at the top, but only enough to adhere one side. Lay out an even row of epoxy, about 1/2 inch (1.3 cm) thick, and as long as the line extending out from the copper T. Place the row of epoxy evenly across the drawn line and next to the copper T. Knead down the epoxy on the bottom of the row to adhere it to the pot. At the top of the row, pinch the epoxy up and away, making a thin-walled trough. Close off the trough where the line ends. While the epoxy is still soft, use a small sharp object to poke holes in the glue. Center the holes in the middle of the trough, and run them down the entire length. Start with small holes approximately 1/8 inch (3 mm) in diameter and 1/2 inch apart. Mix more epoxy and repeat this step on the other side of the copper T. Let the epoxy dry.

testing the water flow

6 Attach the pump to the plastic tubing by flexing the 3 inches (7.6 cm) of tubing up and away from the pot. Cut off some tubing if the pump doesn't sit flat on the bottom of the pot. Fill the pot with enough water to cover the pump's intake valve, plug in the pump cord, and test the water flow. The water should shoot out the three holes in the copper T and run out of the holes made in the epoxy. Adjust the pump pressure for more water flow if desired, or drill larger holes in the epoxy. Don't worry if the water shoots straight out. Rocks will block the holes, and the water will cascade over them.

attaching the rocks

7 Using a wide range of stones—thick, thin, wide, narrow, large, medium, and small—makes it easier to cover the pot and trough. Flat stones work well, as they don't take up much space in the pot. If needed, chisel larger stones down to size. Cover the center of the pot, around the pipe and trough, first. Spread towels on your work surface, and lay the pot on top. Arrange the towels under the pot so it won't roll. First fit the stones inside the pot without glue to determine how many are needed. Place flat pieces of stone with straight edges directly under the epoxy trough. It helps if these stones extend out higher than the trough, allowing other stones to be placed on top to cover the holes.

8 Mix approximately 4 cups (1 L) of the thin set mortar in a bowl. Use the acrylic add mix for extra strength, if desired. Have the water dish and cotton-tipped swabs handy. Apply only a small amount of mortar to each piece of stone. Use more mortar on stones that won't sit flat against the pot, or use narrow, smaller stones instead.

Remove and check the backs of the rocks intended to fill tight spots and curves. Some stones need more mortar to stick in these tricky places.

9 Use a butter knife to apply mortar to the rocks positioned directly under the trough, and set the rocks in place. Build the stones as high as possible along the pot walls until they start to slide or move. Use cotton-tipped swabs dipped in water, or a small hobby stick to clean up excess mortar. Install rocks above the trough and under the light, making sure they don't interfere with or block the channel.

10 Once the top is complete, dry fit rocks to cover one side of the epoxy trough. Find the best-fitting pieces possible. Set more support rocks at the bottom of the trough if needed. Only apply mortar to strategic spots on the trough cover-stones to keep the water holes open. Repeat this process on the second side of the trough. Fill in the rest of the pot using larger stones. Work down the center and up the sides of the pot as high as possible until it's mostly covered. Don't cover the plastic tubing with stones so the pump can be removed and attached without interference. Turn the pot to one side on top of the towel. Mortar more stones to cover all exposed areas. Repeat this process on other side and on the top of the pot if needed. Have the bulb installed in the socket when you surround it with stones. Make sure the bulb can be unscrewed to be replaced. Let the mortar dry.

11 Fill the pot with enough water to cover the pump's intake valve, plug in the pump, and test the water flow. Mortar more stones onto problem areas to correct excessive splash and uneven water flow. If there are only a few trouble spots, adhere the additional stones with epoxy instead of mortar to save time. Keep testing the fountain until the water flow is agreeable. Once you're pleased, disguise the pump and plastic tubing with loose stones.

Panda Paradise

Lush foliage, stately boulders, and a flowing stream make the ideal setting for this happy bear. This successful fountain is as well constructed as it is composed. The panda's bliss is contagious—you'll surely smile with every glance in its direction.

What You Need

Collar, with 3 notches cut for pump cord and water circulation

Round bowl, 4 x 12 inches (10.2 x 30.5 cm)

Decorative rocks

Waterproof epoxy

Chipped slate, assorted sizes

Safety goggles

Dust mask

Work gloves

Variable speed drill

Masonry drill bit, same diameter as tubing

Masonry or rock sealer

Clear plastic tubing, to fit pump spout

*Large rock for panda

Panda figurine

Bamboo, real or artificial

Crystals, optional

Submersible pump

*Select a special rock for your panda's seat. Find one not only large enough to accommodate the bear, but with enough space to simulate a convincing landscape.

2 The fountain head is made from the chipped slate, through which runs the pump's plastic tubing. Make an attractive stack of several slate pieces, approximately 3 inches (7.6 cm) high. Mark each piece to indicate where to drill. Wearing the safety goggles, dust mask, and work gloves, use the masonry bit to drill a hole in each slate piece. Clean all grit from the slate after drilling, let the slate dry, then apply several layers of masonry or rock sealer to each piece according to the manufacturer's instructions.

3 Make the slate stack permanent by gluing its components with waterproof epoxy. As you glue it together, run one end of the plastic tubing three-quarters of the way to the top of the slate. Make sure there's enough plastic tubing at the base of the slate stack to connect to the pump spout. Let the epoxy dry. Glue the underside of the slate stack fountain head to the top edge of the collar.

4 Place the large rock in the bowl with the panda on top to check their combined height. Add small rocks under the panda's rock if it sits too low in the bowl. Glue these elements together with waterproof epoxy.

1 If needed, cut the collar to be flush with or slightly lower than the height of the bowl. Design a multi-layered rock wall to disguise the collar. Extend the wall around the collar for two-thirds to three-quarters of its diameter. Use the waterproof epoxy to glue the rocks to one another, but not to the collar. Allow the epoxy to dry between layers.

5 Determine locations in the bowl for the curved rock wall and the panda's rock. Use the water-proof epoxy to adhere these stationary elements to the base of the bowl, possibly side by side. When the stacked slate fountain head is placed atop the collar, the panda lines up with its interior plastic tubing. Adhere any crystals or artificial plants at this time. In this fountain, one clear crystal sits at the front on the panda's rock, and artificial bamboo lines the rear interior perimeter of the bowl. Let the glued elements dry for at least 24 hours.

6 Adjust the pump's water flow regulator to the lowest setting and center the pump inside the rock wall. Place loose rocks on the base of the bowl in front of the rock wall. Fill the bowl with enough water to cover the pump's intake valve. Position the slate stack fountain head over the pump, connecting the plastic tubing to its spout and running the cord under a notch in the collar. Turn on the pump and rotate the fountain head to achieve the best water flow. Increase the pump pressure and arrange the loose rocks as needed.

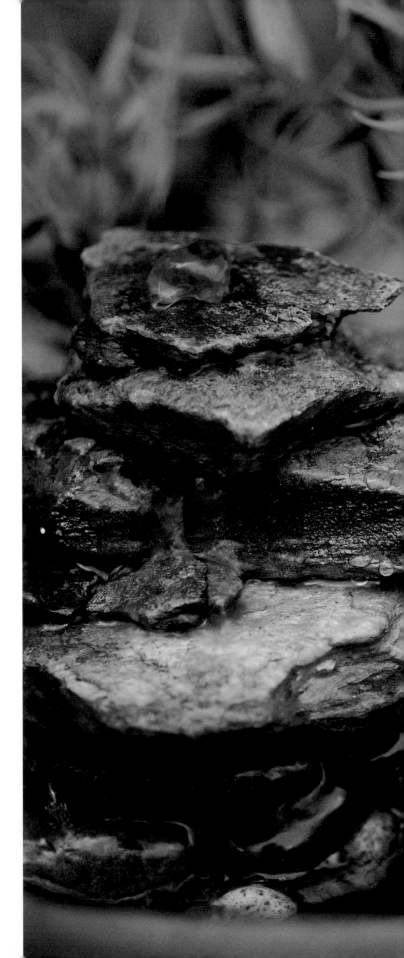

Designer: Tony Estrada

Slate Obelisk

Let the serene beauty of this majestic fountain bring harmony to your home. Rich, multi-hued slate matches the warmth of the wood to form a perfect union. Place a single, extraordinary twig on top of the frame to complete the landscape.

What You Need

*6 slate tiles, each 12 inches (30.5 cm) square; choose 5 tiles with the same thickness, and 1 tile that's considerably thicker

Safety goggles

Hammer

Stone chisel

Clear plastic tubing, 12 inches (30.5 cm) long, to fit pump spout

Thin set mortar, rapid set if available

Acrylic add mix, optional

Butter knife and wooden mixing stick

Small mixing bowl and water bowl

Wax paper, 2 large sheets

String or shoelace

Sandpaper, 100 grit

Cotton-tipped swabs

Waterproof sealer

Wood picture frame, 5 x 7 inches (12.7 x 17.8 cm)

Submersible pump

Waterproof epoxy

Collar with 3 notches for pump cord and water circulation

Variable speed drill

Masonry drill bit, same diameter as plastic tubing

Dust mask and work gloves

Felt or cork pads

 *Try to purchase slate tiles that are flat, with little warping.

preparing the slate

1 On the purchased slate tiles, measure and mark two 8½ x 3½-inch (21.6 x 8.0 cm) rectangles for the front and rear of the fountain base, two 5½ x 3½-inch (14 x 8.9 cm) rectangles for the side base pieces, and one 6¼ x 4¼-inch (15.9 x 10.8 cm) rectangle for the base of the fountain head. The bottom piece of the base will be measured later, once the front, rear, and sides are cut. Bring the marked slate to a tile center and have the pieces cut. Have the rear base piece notched in the center of its top edge for the pump cord. In addition to the marked pieces listed above, have two of the 12-inch (30.5 cm) square slate pieces cut in half—one of the two tiles halved should be the thick one. Save these for the fountain head.

2 Determine where to cut the bottom piece for the base by forming a box on top of it. Lay the bottom piece down and position the front, back, and side pieces. The side lengths fit between the front and back lengths, and all pieces stand on edge. Mark the bottom base piece inside the box along the bottom edges. Number the inside of each base piece to match the bottom piece, so they're easy to reconstruct later. Have the bottom base piece cut. Again, fit the pieces together to make a box without gluing. Check for gaps, and make additional cuts as needed.

creating the fountain head slate

3 The fountain head is constructed of five main parts: three different-sized pieces of chipped slate with a plastic tube sandwiched in between, and a 4 1/4 x 6 1/4-inch (10.8 x 15.9 cm) slate piece for the base. The three chipped pieces are the rear, center, and front. Start with the rear chipped piece, which is the largest of the three. On one of the thinner tile halves cut in Step 1, sketch an attractive chip shape with a 5- to 6-inch width (12.7 to 15.2 cm). Place the piece on a concrete surface. Wearing safety goggles, use a hammer to chisel the shape. Start on the outside edge of the slate and work toward the sketched line in 1/2-inch (1.3 cm) increments to avoid splitting the entire piece.

4 Use one of the thick halved slate tiles for the center chipped piece. Design a shape that is smaller than the rear chipped piece. Chisel this shape as directed in Step 3. The front chipped piece is smaller in width, but the same height as the center chipped piece. Design and chisel the front chipped piece as directed in Step 3. A few extra chipped pieces could be added to the front for a more layered look.

5 Lay down the center chipped piece with its front side facing up. Place the straight length of clear plastic tubing in the center of the slate. Trace along both sides of the tubing with a pen. Chisel between the lines, separating the piece into two parts, to make room for the tube.

assembling the base

6 Mix 2 cups (.5 L) of thin set mortar slightly thicker than the manufacturer's directions. The mortar should have the consistency of thick batter, and barely run off the mixing stick. If desired, use acrylic add mix instead of water for added strength. Place a sheet of wax paper on your work surface and lay the bottom base slate on top. With the butter knife or mixing stick, apply a 1/4- to 1/2-inch (.6 to 1.3 cm) layer of mortar to the rim of the bottom base piece. Too much mortar is better than not enough. Apply mortar to the rear base piece along its interior bottom and side edges. Make sure the pump cord notch is at the top. Press the rear piece firmly in place, corresponding to the number on the bottom piece. The back piece should be centered with its sides sticking out past the bottom piece.

7 Apply mortar to the end edges and to the inside bottom edge of one side piece. Position the side piece on the bottom piece using the corresponding number as a guide. Butt the side piece's end edge to the inside edge of the back piece. Smooth and even out the mortar on the inside joints prior to adding the next two pieces.

8 Mortar and place the final two base pieces, attaching the front piece last. Clean the excess mortar on the outside of the base with a butter knife, then wipe the joints with a damp sponge or rag. Use water sparingly when cleaning mortar. Apply even, firm pressure to all four sides of the base to close any gaps. Tightly tie the slate box together with string, keeping the string centered on the wall of the box. Take up any slack by shimming small pieces of scrap slate between the string and the box. Let the box dry.

assembling the fountain head

9 Mix more mortar if needed. Place the rear chipped piece front side up on a sheet of wax paper. Place the two center pieces front side up on top of the rear piece. Align the bottoms of the slate pieces. Place the plastic tube in the center and 2 inches (5 cm) down from the top of the center piece. Mark this location. Remove the tube and apply mortar to the rear piece in the tube's location, but not past the marked line. Scuff the tube

with the sandpaper and put it in position. Apply a thin layer of mortar to the backside of the center pieces. Clean the channel above the tube with cotton-tipped swabs dabbed in water. Apply mortar to the front piece and press it into position. Clean any excess mortar that was forced out, especially in the channel opening. Align all pieces at their bottom edges so the fountain head sits level. Place a heavy object on top of the fountain head and let it dry.

10 Apply the waterproof sealer to the inside of the slate box and to the wood frame, and let dry. Adjust the submersible pump's water flow regulator to its lowest setting. Place the pump in the center of the box and run the pump cord through the notch. Adhere the wood frame to the top edge of the box with the waterproof epoxy. Cut the collar so the 4$\frac{1}{4}$ x 6$\frac{1}{4}$-inch (10.8 x 15.9 cm) slate piece sits flush with the top of the wood frame.

11 Place the fountain head at the rear of the base. Center the sides and reposition the fountain head until the tubing is 1$\frac{1}{2}$ inches (1.3 cm) from the rear edge. Mark the position of the tubing on the fountain head base. Wearing the safety goggles, dust mask, and work gloves, use a masonry bit to drill a hole at this point.

12 Place the drilled fountain head base on the collar. Feed the tubing from the fountain head through the drilled hole. Cut the plastic tubing enough for the fountain head to sit flat. Mix a small amount of mortar, apply it to the underside of the fountain head, and install the fountain head onto its base. Clean any excess mortar around the joint, using water sparingly. Let the mortar dry.

13 Sand any mortar residue away from the box and the fountain head, then wipe down the elements with a wet rag. Place the felt or cork pads on the bottom corners of the box. Cut the plastic tubing so that when it's attached to the pump, the fountain head sits flat on the collar and the pump sits flat in the box. Cut the tubing in small increments, and check the fit frequently. The easiest way to connect the pump to the tubing is to pick up the pump and slide its spout into the tube while holding the fountain head off the box.

14 Fill the box with enough water to cover the pump's intake valve, and turn on the pump. Adjust the pump pressure as needed. Add a few small pieces of chipped slate around the fountain head.

option

Drill holes in the center of a small stack of the slate chips. Glue them together with waterproof epoxy. This creates a tiny vessel to hold a miniature tree.

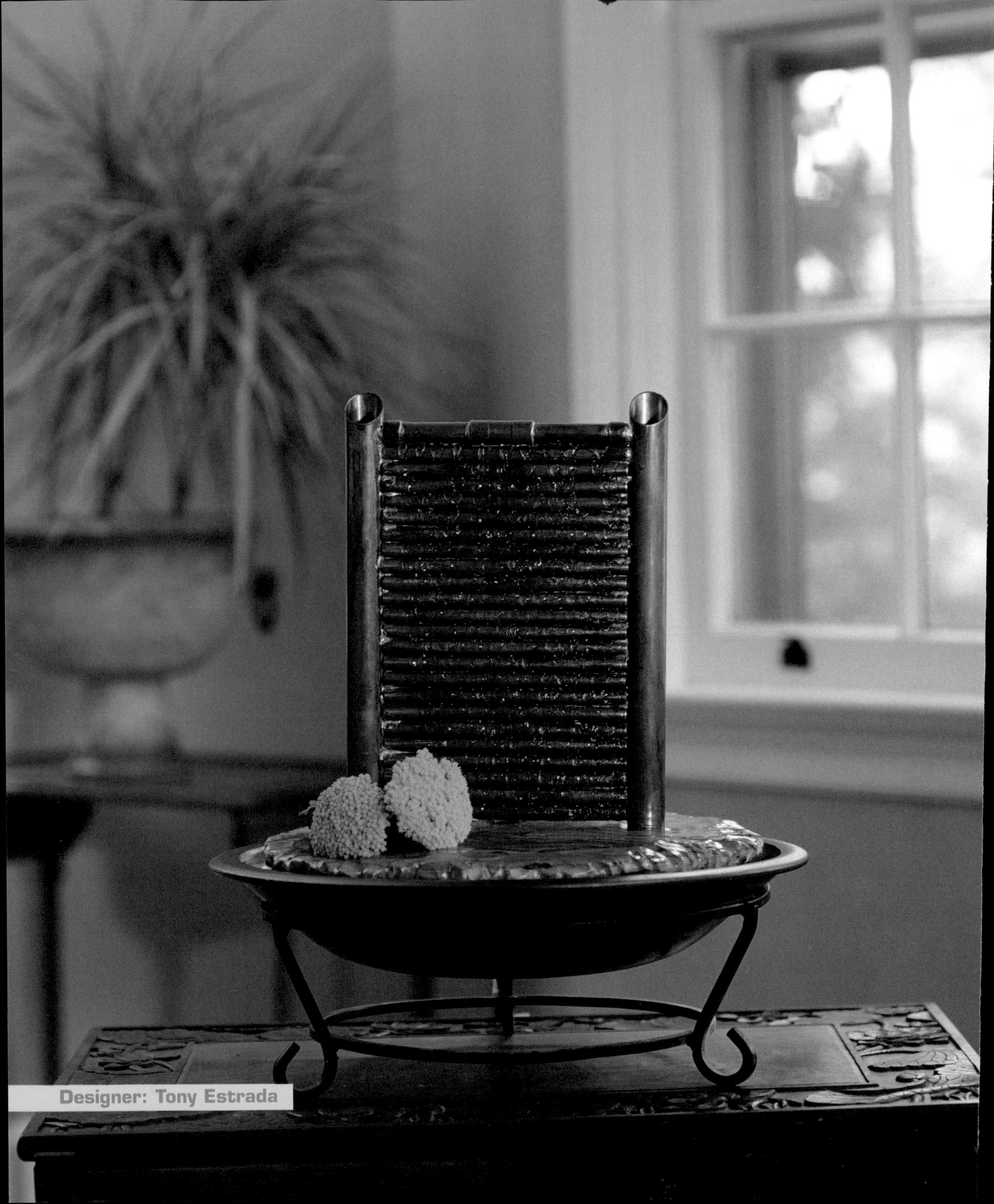

Designer: Tony Estrada

Copper Washboard Fountain

Poised on an end table or pedestal, this sophisticated copper and slate fountain suits any home. Its gentle flow of water lends an atmosphere of serenity. You'll need basic soldering skills to join the pipes, but the result is well worth the extra effort.

What You Need

- Bowl, with a flat base at least 7 $\frac{1}{2}$ inches (17.8 cm) in diameter
- Slate tile, slightly larger than top of bowl
- Collar, with 3 notches for pump cord and water circulation
- Variable speed drill
- Masonry drill bit, same diameter as plastic tube
- Copper pipe, $\frac{3}{8}$ inch (9.5 mm) x 14 feet (4.2 m)
- Pipe cutter or metal hacksaw (miter box is helpful if using hacksaw)
- Copper pipe, $\frac{7}{8}$ x 28 inches (2.2 x 71.1 cm), see Step 4
- Copper pipe, $\frac{1}{2}$ x 24 inches (1.3 x 60.9 cm)
- 2 copper pipe caps, $\frac{1}{2}$ inch (1.3 cm) in diameter
- Copper pipe T adaptor, $\frac{1}{2}$ inch (1.3 cm) in diameter
- Copper pipe elbow adaptor, $\frac{1}{2}$ inch (1.3 cm) in diameter
- Metal drill bit, $\frac{1}{8}$ inch (3 mm) in diameter
- 6 craft or popsicle sticks
- Wooden dowel, $\frac{1}{4}$ x 2 4 inches (.6 x 60.9 cm)
- Plumbing solder
- Propane torch
- Clear plastic tubing, 8 inches (20.3 cm) long, to fit pump spout
- Patina solution, optional
- Submersible pump
- Safety goggles
- Dust mask
- Diamond grinding wheel, small
- Sandpaper

preparing the slate

1 Place the bowl upside down on top of the slate and trace the outline of the bowl. Put the slate on a concrete surface. Wearing the safety goggles and work gloves, chisel the slate to fit inside the top of the bowl. To avoid splitting the slate, begin at one edge and work toward the marked line in $\frac{1}{2}$-inch (1.3 cm) increments. Test fit the chiseled slate by placing the collar in the center of the bowl and resting the slate on top. Reposition or trim the collar with a hacksaw so the slate sits flush with the top of the bowl.

2 Mark the center point of the slate. Wearing the safety goggles, dust mask, and work gloves, use the masonry bit to drill a hole at the mark.

cutting the copper pipe

3 Unroll the $\frac{3}{8}$-inch (9.5 mm) copper pipe, making it as straight as possible. Use a pipe cutter or hacksaw and miter box to cut 23 pieces, each $5\frac{3}{4}$ inches (14.6 cm) long.

Figure 1

cm). Cut one ¾-inch (1.9 cm) length of ½-inch copper pipe, and one 8-inch (20.3 cm) length of ½-inch copper pipe. Cut two 1½-inch (3.8 cm) lengths of ⅜-inch (9.5 mm) copper pipe.

creating the top pipe

6 Clean and solder the copper assembly of two small equal pipe lengths with the copper T and caps created in Step 5. Place one end of the ¾-inch (1.9 cm) length of pipe into the center hole of the T. Place the other end into the elbow. Make sure the elbow is straight, then solder. Once the soldered piece is cool, turn it upside down so the elbow points up. Mark a straight line between the capped ends along the center length of the pipe. Use the ⅛-inch (3 mm) metal bit to drill equally spaced holes along the marked line. (Eleven holes were drilled for this fountain. More can be drilled, or a larger drill bit used, to create a heavier water flow.) If the ⅛-inch bit is slipping off the line, use a smaller bit first to make pilot holes.

soldering the washboard frame

7 Clean the two copper pipes cut in Step 4 at their top, angled ends. The 5¾-inch (14.6 cm) pipe with the drilled holes will join here. Clean the outside ends of the caps again. Lay the two pipes flat, with their angled sides facing straight down. Measure and mark 1 inch (2.5 cm) from the top

4 Measure inside the bowl from its base to the top of the chiseled slate. Add 10 inches (25.4 cm) to this measurement. Cut two pieces of the ⅞-inch (2.2 cm) copper pipe to this length. Cut an angle on one side of both pieces.

5 Cut two small pieces of the ½-inch (1.3 cm) copper pipe to equal lengths. When assembled with the copper T and a cap on each end (see figure 1), the total measurement will equal 5¾ inches (14.6

of each pipe. This is the point where you'll solder the 5¾-inch drilled copper pipe. Hold the drilled pipe by the elbow with the holes facing down, and place it between the two support pipes where the 1-inch marks were made. Put the 8-inch (20.3 cm) pipe cut in Step 5 into the bottom of the elbow. You won't solder this piece. Prop up the drilled pipe so its end caps are centered on the support pipes. Use a set of two stacked craft or popsicle sticks to brace the pipe on both sides. Place the braces between the caps and the T to avoid burning them with the soldering torch. Align the holes on the drilled pipe to allow an evenly centered water flow directly over the next piece of soldered pipe. To achieve this, use any suitable material to prop up the bottom of the 8-inch copper pipe. Place a craft or popsicle stick or rocks under the side of each support pipe to keep it from rolling. Once the layout is correct, solder the pipes together.

arranging and
soldering the washboard pipes

8 Once the piece is cool, remove the 8-inch (20.3 cm) pipe from the elbow. Clean the ends of all twenty-three 5¾-inch (14.6 cm) copper pieces. Clean the inside edge of the two support pipes where the 23 pieces will be soldered. Clean the

backside of the drilled pipe and the two 1½-inch (3.8 cm) lengths of ⅜-inch (9.5 mm) copper pipe. Lay the support pipes angled-side facing down. Cut the wooden dowel in half. Place the two dowels between the support pipes, approximately 3 inches (7.6 cm) apart. Place the first cross pipe

below and touching the bottom of the drilled pipe. Place all remaining cross pipes on top of the dowels. To close any side gaps, wrap a piece of string around the bottom of both support pipes. Reposition the four craft or popsicle sticks under the drilled pipe, and resecure the sides of the support pipes. This protects the soldered pieces at the top of the washboard while the surrounding pipes are heated. Place the two 1½-inch lengths of the ⅜-inch (9.5 mm) copper pipe on top of the seam between the drilled pipe and the first cross pipe. Center these pipes between the copper T and the caps, one on each side. They prevent water from running down the back of the fountain.

9 Solder one side of the washboard at a time, starting at the bottom of the first pipe and working up. Finish a side by soldering the 1½-inch (3.8 cm) pipe at the top. Concentrate on heating one to two pieces at a time when soldering. Solder the second side, working in the same order. Clean and bend a slight curve in the 8-inch (20.3 cm) pipe. The bend moves the pipe closer to the backside of the fountain when the pipe is placed in the elbow. The bend also hides the pipe and improves the side view of the fountain. Place the bent pipe into the elbow and solder. Heat the elbow with just the tip of the flame to avoid overheating the surrounding soldered pieces. Sand the piece to make it shiny, or apply a patina solution if desired. Liver of sulfur was used to finish this fountain.

10 Slide the plastic tubing over the pump spout and form a tight seal. Adjust the water flow regulator to its lowest setting. Place the pump and collar in the center of the bowl. Feed the plastic tube through the slate's center hole, and rest the slate on the collar. Position the copper washboard so the bent 8-inch (20.3 cm) copper pipe is aligned with the plastic tube. Trace the outline of the two support pipes in position on the slate. Remove the slate from the fountain. Wearing the safety goggles, dust mask, and work gloves, use the masonry bit to drill the marked holes. Grind out the rest of the hole using the small diamond grinding bit. Make sure the support pipes fit tightly in the holes. If you remove too much slate, add a bit of epoxy to the inside of the hole.

11 Fill the bowl with enough water to cover the pump's intake filter. Replace the slate on the collar and tubing. Slide the two support pipes into the holes in the slate. Cut the plastic tube and slide it a few inches onto the copper pipe. Add decorative stones or plants if desired.

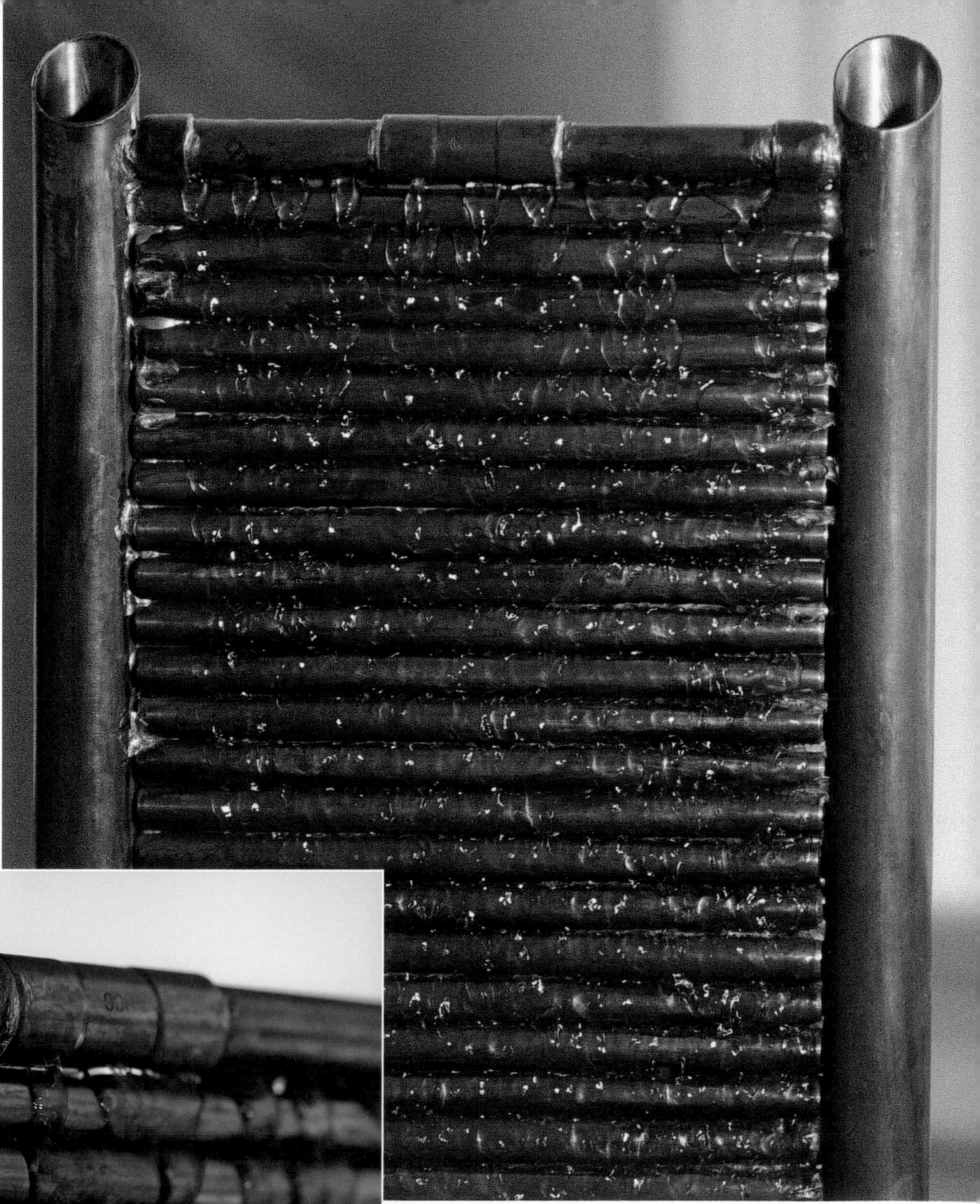

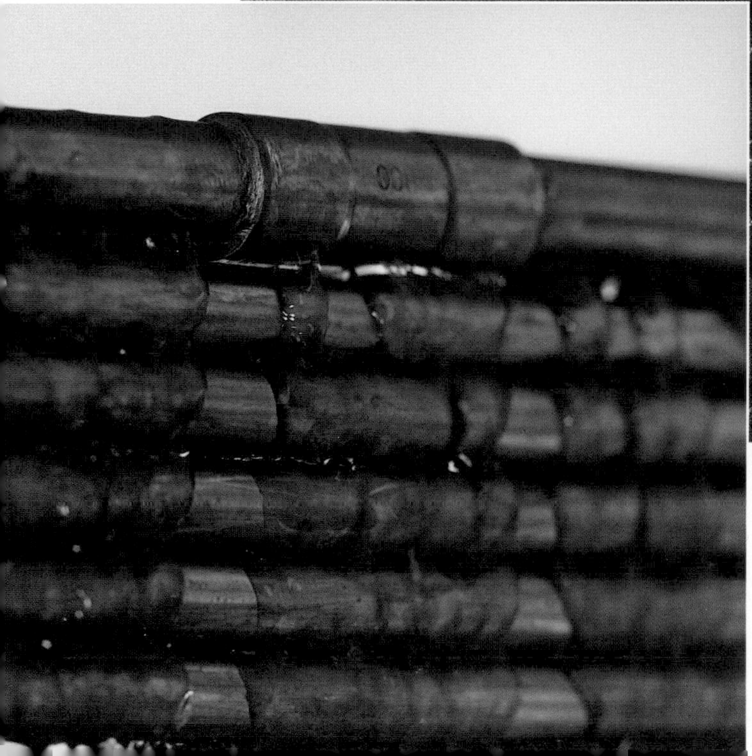

Daisy Dream

Water positively glistens as it tumbles down the carved facade of this lovely slate fountain. Having the slate professionally cut at a tile center saves you time and labor. Carving the daisy and floral border by hand is a great way to exercise your imagination and reveal the inner beauty of the slate.

What You Need

*7 slate tiles, each 12 inches (30.5 cm) square

Small motorized rotary tool

Small diamond carving bits, disc-shaped and pointed

Photocopied template of daisy pattern, page 120

Sandpaper, 100-grit

Waterproof epoxy

Thin set mortar, rapid set if available

Acrylic add mix, optional

Wax paper, 2 large sheets

Old butter knife or wooden mixing stick

Small mixing bowl and water bowl

Submersible pump

Plastic bag, sandwich size

Cotton-tipped swabs

Shoelace or string, 45 inches (114 cm) long

Variable speed drill

Masonry drill bit, same diameter as tubing

Collar, with 3 notches for pump cord and water circulation

Clear plastic tubing, 10 inches (25.4 cm) long, to fit pump spout

Waterproof masonry sealer

Silicone, optional

Gloss exterior varnish

Very small hobby paintbrush

Felt or cork pads

River stones

*Try to purchase slate tiles that are flat, with little warping, and are the same thickness.

preparing the slate

1 On one slate tile measure and mark a 10-inch (25.4 cm) square. Mark another 6 ¼-inch (15.9 cm) square in the center of the first square. This will be cut out to make a frame.

2 On other slate tiles, measure and mark two 3 ¾ x 7 ½-inch (9.5 x 19 cm) rectangles, two 3 ¾ x 6 ½-inch (9.5 x 16.5 cm) rectangles, two 5 ½ x 10-inch (14 x 25.4 cm) rectangles, and two 1 ¼ x 10-inch (3.2 x 25.4 cm) rectangles. Reserve one whole slate tile for the base. It will be measured once the side pieces are cut.

3 Bring all the marked slate to a tile center and have the pieces cut. Place the reserved base piece on a flat surface. Stand the cut pieces on edge to form a box on top of the base slate. The 3 ¾ x 7 ½-inch (9.5 x 19 cm) pieces are the front and back of the box and the 3 ¾ x 6 ½-inch (9.5 x 16.5 cm) pieces are the sides. Fit the shorter lengths between the longer lengths. Mark the base slate on the inside of the box along its bottom edges. Number the inside of each box piece to match the base piece, so they're easily reassembled later. Have the base slate cut to the marks made above.

4 Fit all the cut slate pieces together by re-making the box and placing the 10-inch (25.4 cm) square slate piece on top. Determine which

3 ¾ x 7 ½-inch (9.5 x 19 cm) piece will be the back. Wearing the safety goggles, dust mask, and work gloves, use the rotary tool with the diamond grinding bit to carve out a notch for the electrical cord at the top of the back piece.

5 Select one of the 10 x 5 ½-inch (25.4 x 14 cm) slate rectangles to be the front of the fountain head. Measure and mark ½ inch (1.3 cm) down from its top edge and 2 ⅛ inches (5.4 cm) on either side of its center point. Wearing the safety goggles, dust mask, and work gloves, use the diamond bit on the motorized rotary tool to carve out this area. A cutting disc works best to make this indentation.

creating the daisy and the border

6 Cut out the daisy template (see figure 1) to make a stencil. Position the stencil on top of the fountain

Figure 1

head's front piece, and trace the outline of the stencil. Draw a simple floral border around the perimeter of the 10-inch (25.4 cm) square slate piece. This fountain only has side and front borders.

7 Wearing the safety goggles, dust mask, and work gloves, use the motorized rotary tool with the small pointed diamond bit to carve the daisy feature and floral border. If desired, practice carving on scrap slate first to build your skill. Select a medium setting for the rotary tool. Experiment with different size diamond bits for different effects. A diamond wheel works best for the daisy petals and leaves.

constructing a barrier in the fountain head

8 Lay down the rear fountain head piece (5½ x 10 inches [14 x 25.4 cm]) on a flat surface. Place the two 1¼ x 10-inch (3.2 x 25.4 cm) side pieces on edge at opposite sides of the rear piece. Scuff the clear plastic tubing with the sandpaper. Place the tube in the center of the rear piece, 2 inches (5 cm) down from its top edge. Make a mark across the top of the slate where the tube ends. Also mark the bottom edge where the tube runs off the slate. Mix the waterproof epoxy and make a barrier around the top of the tubing (see figure 2). Wet the inside surface of the side pieces to keep them from sticking to the epoxy. Wet a flat piece of scrap slate. Use this as a tool to flatten

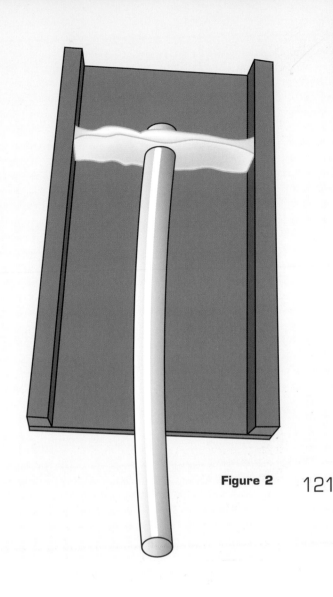

Figure 2

121

the top of the epoxy. This creates a barrier, keeping the water from running back into the fountain head. Remove the thin side pieces and let the epoxy dry.

building the base

9 Mix 2 cups (.5 L) of thin set mortar slightly thicker than the manufacturer's directions. It should have the consistency of thick batter and barely run off the mixing stick. Use the acrylic add mix instead of water for additional strength if desired. Place the wax paper on your work surface. Apply a $\frac{1}{4}$- to $\frac{1}{2}$-inch (.6 to 1.3 cm) layer of mortar to the rim of the bottom base piece with the butter knife or mixing stick. Too much mortar is better than not enough. Apply the mortar to the back piece along its inside bottom edge and sides. Press it firmly in place, using the corresponding number on the bottom piece as a guide, so it's centered with its sides sticking out. Apply mortar to the outside ends and to the inside bottom of one side piece. Position it adjacent to the corresponding number on the bottom piece, and butt the end to the inside edge of the back. Smooth and even out the mortar on the inside joints before adding the next two pieces. Try not to take away too much mortar when smoothing. Continue to mortar the other two pieces starting with the front, and then the remaining side. Clean the excess mortar on the outside using the butter knife, and wipe with a damp sponge or rag. Apply firm and even pressure to all four sides to close any gaps. Apply mortar to the top edge of the front, back, and side pieces.

122

10 Put the pump in a sandwich-size plastic storage bag, and place it in the center of the mortared slate box. Fit the pump cord through the notch in the back slate piece. Place the 10-inch (25.4 cm) square slate piece on top of the box. Remove any excess mortar on the inside, and smooth it with

your finger. Use cotton-tipped swabs dipped in water to clean up the outside of the joint. Tie the string around all four sides of the box, keeping it in the middle of the slate. Make as tight a knot as possible. To take up slack, use small scraps of slate as shims between the string and the slate. Once dry, use the sandpaper to clean up any mortar residue.

assembling the fountain head

11 Mix additional mortar as described in Step 9. Lay down a second sheet of wax paper and place the rear fountain head piece on top. Apply the mortar to both inside edges of the rear piece where the two side pieces will attach. Add a small amount of

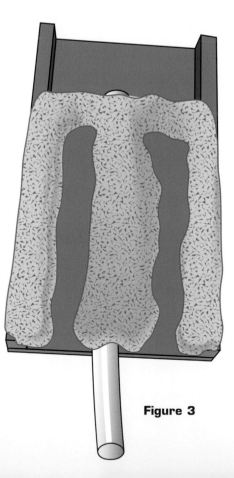

Figure 3

the mortar to the sides of the epoxy barrier. Set the two 1¼-inch (3.2 cm) side pieces firmly into the mortar. Make sure the side piece edges (top, bottom, and sides) are all flush with the edges of the rear piece. Wipe away any excess mortar on the inside of the seam above the water barrier. Apply generous amounts of mortar below the water barrier and along the length of the tube (see figure 3).

12 Lay the front piece daisy-side down on top of the wax paper. Apply mortar to the inside edges of the front piece where it joins the side pieces. Place the front piece on top of the side pieces. Clean up any excess mortar, especially around the top interior. The bottom of the tubing should be in the center of the width of the front and back pieces. This helps later when drilling the tubing hole.

13 On the 6-inch (15.2 cm) square slate piece cut from the 10-inch (25.4 cm) square frame, measure and mark a point 2 inches (5 cm) from the rear and 3⅛ inches (8 cm) from the side. Wearing the safety goggles, dust mask, and work gloves, use the masonry bit to drill a hole at this point the same diameter as the plastic tubing. Drill slowly with caution to avoid breaking or splitting the slate.

14 Cut the collar so the fountain head base slate sits approximately ¼ inch (6 mm) below the base frame.

15 Mix ½ cup (12 mL) of mortar as described in Step 9. Place the fountain head base on top of the collar. Apply a generous amount of mortar to the underside of the fountain head. Slide the tubing through the hole in the fountain head and press down firmly. Clean excess mortar away from the joint with a sponge or rag. Allow the mortar to dry.

16 Remove the pump from the plastic bag and place it and the collar in the center of the base. Cut the bottom of the plastic tubing to a length that, when connected to the pump spout, lets the fountain head sit flat on the collar, and the pump sit flat on the base. Cut the tubing in small increments and check the fitting often. The easiest way to connect the pump is to pick it up and slide its spout into the tube while holding up the fountain head.

123

17 Place the pump on top of the base frame edge. Apply the masonry waterproof sealer to the interior of the base. Let the sealer dry. Apply epoxy or silicone around the pump cord hole and let it dry. Paint the daisy and floral border with the gloss exterior finish. Attach the felt or cork pads to the bottom corners of the base. Place the collar back in the center of the base. Fill the base with enough water to cover the pump's intake filter. Attach the pump to the fountain head, and rest it on the collar. Turn on the pump. Arrange polished stones in front of the fountain head if desired. Adjust the pump pressure as needed.

suiseki

The idea of collecting and displaying rocks just for their aesthetic appeal might seem a little odd to a Westerner—but what child hasn't pocketed pretty pebbles as treasures to take home and display on a shelf or nightstand?

what is it?

For thousands of years, Chinese and Japanese collectors have sought out *suiseki,* stones possessing two prized qualities: suggestive shape and beauty. The name literally means "water stone" and derives from the ancient custom of displaying landscape stones in trays filled with water, as well as the shaping of the stone by the erosive action of water. Suiseki is also often translated as "viewing stones." These unworked stones suggest natural shapes such as mountains, waterfalls or crags, and even whole landscapes. Sometimes placed in bonsai pots, suiseki are also appreciated alone.

124

The U.S. National Arboretum in Washington, D.C. has a permanent collection of suiseki, as does the Crespi Bonsai Center in Milan, Italy. Many bonsai exhibitions feature suiseki in their displays.

origins

Historians believe the art originated in China about two thousand years ago; in the sixth century, emissaries brought several suiseki to Japan. Reflecting the Chinese taste of the period, these stones often had fantastical shapes, deep folds and hollows, highly eroded surfaces, and holes. The Japanese appreciated not only the natural beauty of the stones, but also their religious and philosophical symbolism.

As time passed and tastes in Japan changed, suiseki attained stricter levels of refinement and perfection. Under the influence of Zen Buddhism, collectors sought out a different type of stone. They prized stones that were subtle, serene, austere, and unpretentious. Reduced to their barest essentials, the stones became a means to spiritual refinement, inner awareness, and enlightenment. Connoisseurs held gatherings to show their suiseki (some highly prized stones had specially designed travel cases!), and competed with one another to write verse about the stones on display. The Japanese often gave poetic and evocative names to their suiseki, such as "Floating Bridge of Dreams" or "Moon Over the Rice Paddies."

display

Suiseki are usually displayed in a hardwood stand, called a *dai,* which is carved to snugly fit the bottom of the stone. Collectors also display their stones in a *suiban,* a shallow tray with no holes in the bottom. In this case, the stone sits in either sand or water.

classifications

Suiseki are classified by shape, color, and surface pattern. Shape is the most common classification, defining scenic landscape and object stones. Scenic landscape stones include stones evocative of natural topography such as mountains, islands, caves, slopes, and coastal rocks; waterfall stones have a vein of a lighter color that appears to be a waterfall. Object stones resemble things like humans, animals, houses, or bridges. Apart from solid colors, there is also a classification for five-color stones. Surface patterns can look like humans, animals, plants, or landscapes. Some suiseki have celestial patterns, or motifs reminiscent of weather.

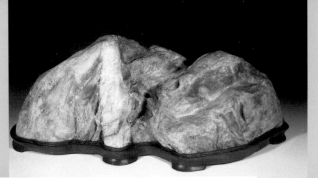

Select smoothly eroded stones: freshly fractured stones do not convey the required sense of antiquity and mellowness. The stones should have balance, created by the dynamic interplay of opposing yet complementary aspects. Asymmetrical elements combine to create a harmonious whole: tall/short, rough/smooth, convex/concave.

At first it might seem difficult to pick out a stone from among thousands. When you spot a potential stone, look it over from all sides to consider how it would look on display. Some collectors specialize in a particular type of stone, while others aim to have at least one high-quality sample from each major suiseki classification. Fervent collectors traditionally keep records on their suiseki's origin, such as where they were found, their mineral content and rock type, previous owners, and other related information.

preparation

After collecting the stones, wash them. Remove the bulk of dirt under a jet of water, then soak the stones for a half hour with a few drops of detergent. If needed, use a plastic brush or steel brush to remove any persistent grime. Brush slowly and gently to avoid damaging your suiseki. Dry the stones with a towel or in the sun.

Remember the cardinal rule: suiseki should remain the way that natural forces shaped them. Never lacquer or varnish them. The luster of the stone due to natural polishing by water can be enhanced by hand rubbing with a little oil, but this will take years of devotion.

in your fountain

In a fountain, you might display a lone suiseki on a slab of slate with water gently rippling across the surface. Alternately, you could put it in a shallow sand- or water-filled ceramic dish placed on the slate. Experiment with the size and shape of the dish as well as the placement of the suiseki within it. The suiseki could also be placed atop a cube of treated wood in an otherwise empty fountain. Aim for simplicity and a minimum of elements.

did you know?

selection

What makes a suiseki different from ordinary stones? A pleasing shape, a tasteful display, and the feeling that the stone has something more. Look for stones with an appealing shape and texture, and that suggest a mountain, waterfall, or other natural scene. The stone should be larger than a jewel or pendant, but not too heavy to lift. Anything larger is considered an outdoor garden stone. Choose hard, firm stones with a subdued color that comes from deep within the rock (although outside of Japan, lightweight volcanic or sedimentary stones have gained popularity in recent years). Paradoxically, it often seems that the simpler the stone, the greater its expressive possibilities.

contributing designers

paris mannion pursued graduate studies in medieval and modern European History at Rutgers University during the 1960s. After graduation, while on a four-week college tour of England, France, Italy, and Germany, she photographed six outdoor fountains with plumes of water jetting into the air. At the time, she thought of them as unusual pieces of architecture, but didn't realize that decades later her interest would lead to teaching fountain building.

A resident of San Diego, California, Mannion has been a licensed therapist since 1982, and a professional coach since 1996. Her clients often build fountains as a tool for reflection, balance, and harmony. She has authored two books on building tabletop fountains, and leads fountain classes at adult education centers. View Paris' website at www.BuildFountains.com.

alan d. otterson's hobbies and interests (besides fountain building) include astronomy, archaeology, computers, photography, and the paranormal. He and his wife reside in Michigan, his native state.

tony estrada discovered his talent for building fountains in 1999 when he made them as Christmas gifts for his friends and family. His love of nature and the outdoors inspires his designs. Estrada lives in Southern California. View Tony's website at www.wetrockcreations.com.

126

todd browning began making fountains in 1994 so he could hear the sound of water in his daily life. An avid backpacker, scuba diver, and gem lover, Browning combines elements of these interests into his fountains. He designs with the goal of bringing indoors the energy and beauty of the outdoors. View Todd's website at www.indoorenergies.com.

nancy carr's inspiration for her fountain designs comes from living amongst the wildlife in the Sierra Mountains of California. She has had a life-long interest in art, and has won numerous awards. She makes and sells scenic wildlife fountains at craft fairs, and has created displays for home and garden shows. You can e-mail Nancy at mtngal@goldrush.com.

susan kieffer has enjoyed dabbling in crafts all of her life. She lived in the Florida Keys for many years, but traded the sea for the mountains of Asheville, North Carolina, where she currently works as assistant editor for *Fiberarts* magazine.

terry taylor is a prolific designer with widely ranging interests, from jewelry making to candle decorating. He lives in Asheville, North Carolina, where he is an editor and writer at Lark Books.

A special thanks to the talented designers who made this book possible: Tony Estrada, Todd Browning, Paris Mannion, Susan Kieffer, Nancy Carr, Alan D. Otterson, and Terry Taylor. Their passionate dedication to fountains is inspiring.

acknowledgments

Elaine Nobriga generously provided many of the fountain supplies photographed for this book. Please visit Elaine's excellent website at www.fountainbuilder.com.

Fantastic photography locations were provided by Betty Lou Jeffrey, Jane and Bob Collins, Sara and Gerald Le Van, Stephanie Smith, and Sandra Stambaugh and Peter Alberice. Thank you for such a warm welcome into your homes!

Felix Rivera, of the California Suiseki Society, furnished the outstanding suiseki photographs. Thank you for your kindness and commitment to this intriguing art form.

Dawn Cusick, a fountain of fountain wisdom, was frequently called upon. She not only contributed her knowledge and experience, but made this adventure great fun!

Rick Morris lent his design insight and technical expertise to the fountains that I made for this book. Thanks for your boundless energy and constant support.

127

index